BEYOND LIBERALISM
AND FUNDAMENTALISM

THE ROCKWELL LECTURE SERIES
WERNER H. KELBER, GENERAL EDITOR

The Rockwell Lectures constitute the oldest designated and now endowed lecture series at Rice University, Houston, Texas. Since 1938, when the inaugural lecture was delivered, the Rockwell Fund has generously supported the series. The lectures are dedicated to the general subject of religion.

In the series:

Beyond Liberalism and Fundamentalism
by Nancey Murphy

Christianity and Civil Society
by Robert Wuthnow

BEYOND LIBERALISM AND FUNDAMENTALISM

How Modern and Postmodern Philosophy
Set the Theological Agenda

Nancey Murphy

TRINITY PRESS INTERNATIONAL
VALLEY FORGE, PENNSYLVANIA

Trinity Press International, P.O. Box 851, Valley Forge, PA 19482-0851
Trinity Press International is part of the Morehouse Publishing Group.

Library of Congress Cataloging-in-Publication Data

Murphy, Nancey C.
  Beyond liberalism and fundamentalism : how modern and postmodern philosophy set the theological agenda / Nancey Murphy.
    p.   cm.
  Includes bibliographical references.
  ISBN 1-56338-176-1 (alk. paper)
  1. Theology—History—20th century.   2. Theology-Methodology.
3. Philosophy, Modern.   4. Philosophy and religion.   5. Language and languages—Religious aspects.   6. Liberalism (Religion)—Protestant churches.   7. Conservatism—Religious aspects.   I. Title.
BT28.M87   1996
261.5'1'0904—dc20   96-24736
                                                                CIP

Ediset by Joan Marie Laflamme
Printed in the United States of America

96 97 98 99 00 01 02 7 6 5 4 3 2 1

to my parents

Richard and Shirley Murphy

Contents

Preface

My career in theological academia has been rather varied in that I received my theological education at an institution identified with the liberal side of American Christianity (The Graduate Theological Union, Berkeley, California), yet have taught for a number of years in a conservative seminary (Fuller Theological Seminary, Pasadena, California). As an explorer of this varied theological landscape, I offer some amateurish sociological observations:

- Inhabitants of liberal territory tend to believe that the Christian world is made up only of themselves and fundamentalists.
- Evangelicals are seen by fundamentalists to have slid down the slippery slope to liberalism.
- There are often deeper divisions between liberals and conservatives within a denomination than there are between one denomination and another.
- Postliberal theologians appear as fideists to liberals but as relativists to conservatives.

These misunderstandings and disagreements, some amusing and others almost tragic, are comparable to the disagreements and communication failures that the late Thomas Kuhn recognized in the history of science. Adherents of competing paradigms in science tend to talk past one another, even to dismiss one another's work as "not real science."

The thesis of this book is that modern theologians have managed to develop two quite different theological "paradigms." As a consequence, conservatives often fail to understand what liberal theologians are saying. My suspicion is that many conservative Christians focus on superficial disagreements and are unaware of just how deep the differences are between their understandings of Christianity and the positions of the liberals. While it is certainly possible for fundamentalists to "slide down the slippery slope" to evangelicalism, it is not equally possible to slide from evangelicalism to liberalism. There is an invisible wall in between; a "paradigm shift" is required.

This same paradigm analysis accounts for the fact that "evangelical theology" sounds like an oxymoron to liberals.

The divide between liberal and conservative in American Protestantism is news to no one. What I hope to do in this book is to help explain the source of this divide. In brief, modern *philosophical* assumptions provided limited options to theologians if their work was to make sense in the modern world. On a number of issues—justification of theological claims, the nature of religious language, accounts of divine action—there have been only two viable strategies. Choice of one or the other of these sets of options produces a distinctively liberal or distinctively conservative theology.

The differences between liberal and conservative theologies, however, are less significant that those between modern thinkers of all sorts and those who have adopted the standpoint of a new intellectual world in the making, which I label Anglo-American postmodernity. At present this shift in philosophical assumptions is creating even deeper levels of misunderstanding than between modern liberals and conservatives. Yet I make the claim, perhaps startling to some, that this revolution offers hope for a rapprochement between Christians of the left and right. Constructive dialogue is already taking place between postliberals and "postmodern evangelicals."[1] I hope to contribute to this movement in the second half of the book by describing these new philosophical positions and suggesting how theology might develop in response.

I was stimulated to begin this project by an invitation to give the Rockwell Lectures at Rice University in 1994. My thanks to the donors, to Werner Kelber, then chair of the religion department, and to the graduate students who took time for meals and conversation.

I was pleased to learn that Trinity Press International would be publishing the lecture series: it is a delight to work with Hal Rast and Laura Barrett there.

Thanks, also, to friends and colleagues who read part or all of the book and offered helpful suggestions: Brad Kallenberg, James M. Smith, Robert John Russell, Rosalee Velloso. Charles Scalise and my husband, James Wm. McClendon, Jr., were especially helpful.

---

[1] See, for example, *The Nature of Confession: Evangelicals and Postliberals in Conversation*, ed. Timothy R. Phillips and Dennis Okholm (Downers Grove, IL: InterVarsity Press, 1996).

BEYOND LIBERALISM
AND FUNDAMENTALISM

Introduction

OVERVIEW

American Protestant Christianity is often described as a two party system. The division between "liberals" and "conservatives" (including both fundamentalists and evangelicals) is a deep one, and often marked by acrimony and stereotypes.[1] I leave it to the sociologists and historians to account for the acrimony.[2] My goal here is to help clarify the differences between the intellectual positions of these two groups and to advance the thesis that the *philosophy* of the modern period is largely responsible for the bifurcation of Protestant Christian thought.[3]

A second thesis of the book is that the modern philosophical positions that drove this division have all been called into question. So it is time to ask how theology ought to be done in a *post*modern era and to envision a rapprochement between theologians of the left and right.

In Part I of the book we shall look at various modern philosophical positions regarding knowledge and language, and at the modern determinist worldview based on the physical sciences, and examine the consequences of all of these for theology. My thesis is that in each case philosophical assumptions provided limited options for theologians if they were to do their work in a way that made sense in the modern world. In fact, theologians were presented with several pairs of options. Choice of one or the other option, in each case, produced a characteristically liberal or conservative theology.

In Part II we survey criticisms of modern philosophy, along with the developing postmodern positions, and consider the consequences of the new philosophy for theology.

---

1. See Roger E. Olson, "Whales and Elephants: Both God's Creatures But Can They Meet? Evangelicals and Liberals in Dialogue," *Pro Ecclesia* 4, no. 2: 165-89.

2. See, for example, Robert Wuthnow, *The Restructuring of American Religion, Society and Faith Since World War II* (Princeton: Princeton University Press, 1988); George Marsden, *Understanding Fundamentalism and Evangelicalism* (Grand Rapids, MI: Eerdmans, 1991); and Martin E. Marty, *Modern American Religion, Volume 2: The Noise and the Conflict, 1919-1941* (Chicago: University of Chicago Press, 1991).

3. I shall concentrate on Protestant thought here, but similar distinctions could be drawn within the Catholic fold, as well.

Chapter 1 explains two central aspects of modern philosophical views of knowledge: First, foundationalism is the theory of knowledge, based on the metaphor of knowledge as a building, that requires all beliefs to be justified by tracing them to a special category of beliefs that cannot be called into question. My thesis is that foundationalism has contributed to the split between liberal and conservative theologies by forcing theologians to choose Scripture or experience as the source of this special, foundational class of beliefs. Conservatives have chosen Scripture; liberals, characteristically, have chosen experience.

A second feature of most modern philosophical theories of knowledge is their "inside-out" character.[4] That is, they begin with the contents of the mind of the knowing subject and attempt to argue from those inner representations to conclusions about the character of the external world. We shall see that liberal theologians tend to be inside-out thinkers, while conservatives take an outside-in approach.

Chapter 2 presents two modern theories of language. The dominant theory is the representational or referential theory; it has been adapted for use by conservative theologians, whose view of religious and theological language is generally called *propositional*. A secondary theory of language may be called *expressivist*, and this theory applies to liberal views of religious language.

The split between liberals and conservatives on religious language corresponds with a split over the issue of how theology or religion relates to other knowledge, especially to science. The expressivist view of religious language allows theology and science to be seen as non-interacting views of reality, while the propositionalist view of religious language requires that theology and science be viewed as capable of overlap and conflict—each making its contribution to a single description of reality.

Chapter 3 traces the connections within a set of concepts that characterize the modern worldview: atomism, reductionism, and determinism. These are philosophical or "metaphysical" positions that derive their power from early modern science. Their consequences for theology relate to the problem of divine action: if the physical processes in the universe are strictly determined by the laws of physics, then how does God act? The two typical responses have been the liberal view that God acts in and through natural processes (which I shall call *immanentism*) and the conservative view—*interventionism*—that God is able and willing to violate or suspend the laws of nature in order to bring about special revelatory and providential events.

Also in Chapter 3 we look at the ways both sets of options, the liberal and the conservative, form a coherent account of the nature and methods of

---

4. This term comes from Wallace Matson. See *A New History of Philosophy*, 2 vols. (San Diego, CA: Harcourt Brace Jovanovich, 1987), 2:275-76.

theology. That is, the choice a theologian makes regarding divine action has important implications for choices on other issues: an immanentist view calls for an experiential approach to theological foundations *and* an expressivist view of religious language; an interventionist account allows for a scriptural foundation for theology *and* a propositional view of religious language.

Chapter 4 sums up the criticisms that have led philosophers to reject foundationalism and describes the developing "holist" approaches to epistemology, from W. V. O. Quine to Alasdair MacIntyre. We examine some of the uses theologians have made of holism and also look ahead to possible further developments.

Chapter 5 examines the postmodern theories of language of Ludwig Wittgenstein and J. L. Austin and looks at their consequences for giving an account of theological and religious language. It also considers implications for biblical studies.

Chapter 6 looks at changes in science that have called the reductionist and determinist view of nature into question. It presents a new view of the relations among the sciences, and of the sciences to theology, that goes a great distance toward answering the modern problem of divine action.

In the Conclusion I speculate on how differences between today's liberals and conservatives might play out in the era now dawning. I claim that while there will be a spectrum of theological positions from left to right, there will be no intellectual compulsion to bifurcate the spectrum into two discrete camps.

WHY PHILOSOPHY?

I am making strong claims for the role of philosophy in theological development, which will be surprising to many. The justification for my claims can only come from the success of the arguments that follow, but it may be helpful to say a bit here about the nature of philosophy, and thereby provide some rationale for expecting philosophy to have a great deal of relevance to theology. In brief, the rationale is based on the relation philosophy bears to the rest of culture. Huston Smith has written:

> The dominant assumptions of an age color the thoughts, beliefs, expectations, and images of the men and women who live within it. Being always with us, these assumptions usually pass unnoticed—like the pair of glasses which, because they are so often on the wearer's nose, simply stop being observed. But this doesn't mean they have no effect. Ultimately, assumptions which underlie our outlooks on life refract the world in ways that condition our art and our institutions: the kinds of homes we live in, our sense of right and wrong, our criteria of success, what we conceive our duty to be, what we think it means

to be a man or woman, how we worship our God or whether, indeed, we have a God to worship.[5]

A central task of philosophy is to expose these often invisible assumptions, to criticize them, to suggest improvements or replacements; these new theories often become the assumptions upon which the next era of scholarship is based. Thus, philosophy helps us sum up the most basic characteristics of an era past and foreshadows features of the era to come.

We might say that philosophy is the discipline that studies (and makes recommendations for changing) the very *materials* that theologians must use for their thinking. We can distinguish between the content of Christian theology and the categories, concepts, forms of arguments that theologians have available for discussing and warranting that content. Although this distinction between content and categories is not a hard and fast one, we can think of the content of theology as coming from its own special sources (for example, revelation), while the concepts and forms of arguments are the province of philosophy.

PERIODIZATION

I have been speaking of "the modern period," and my mention of "postmodern" developments in philosophy implies that the modern period may be coming to an end. It is notoriously difficult to draw sharp boundaries between one historical era and another. There are always continuities as well as changes, and the changes that represent shifts from one era to another do not come at the same time in all disciplines or in all geographic regions. Philosophers, however, are in rather close agreement that René Descartes was the first modern philosopher, and so the date of his death in 1650 is often used to date the beginning of modern philosophy.

Notice that I have been looking at philosophy in order to date the beginning of modernity. If we looked at theology instead the dates would be different. Friedrich Schleiermacher is often called the first modern theologian, and the publication of *On Religion: Speeches to Its Cultured Despisers* gives us 1799 as a crucial date for the beginning of modern theology—150 years later!

If we looked at science, we might want to use 1632, the date of the publication of Galileo's *Dialogue Concerning the Two Chief World Systems,* as the beginning of modernity, for the Copernican revolution was the beginning of the end of the medieval worldview.

---

5. Huston Smith, *Beyond the Post-Modern Mind,* 2d ed. (Wheaton, IL: The Theosophical Publishing House, 1989), 3-4.

In a variety of disciplines, now, including art and architecture, literature, philosophy, and science, authors are claiming that the modern era is over, and that we have entered a new, postmodern period.[6] However, the term *postmodern* is highly contested, and it is not clear that any common meaning can be found in its application to this wide variety of fields. The most common use of the term applies to a movement in literary criticism, deconstructionism, which has grown out of French structuralism, but that is not our use here. Rather, in Part II, I describe what I take to be postmodern positions in Anglo-American philosophy. Since these positions began to be formulated around 1950, this makes a convenient date for the end of the modern period and the beginning of the postmodern period in philosophy. Furthermore, if what I have said above about the intimate relation between philosophy and other aspects of culture is correct, it is not unreasonable to date the modern period itself from 1650 to 1950. Of course, intellectual periods never end abruptly; we are very much in transition now from one way of viewing knowledge, language, reality to another.

The philosophers who will concern us in Part I are René Descartes (1596-1650), John Locke (1632-1704), David Hume (1711-1776), Thomas Reid (1710-1796), and Immanuel Kant (1724-1804). Their relations to one another and to theological developments are shown below.

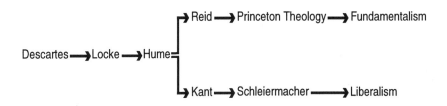

This sketch represents the following intellectual dependencies: Locke took Descartes's foundationalist view of knowledge, modified it somewhat, and applied it to religious knowledge. Hume is important in this historical sequence because of his skeptical arguments that called into question Locke's positive theories of both scientific and religious knowledge. Reid and Kant each responded to Hume's skepticism in his own way, and in so doing each provided philosophical resources for the development of a theological tradition—Reid for American fundamentalists by means of his influence on theologians such as Charles Hodge, his son Archibald Alexander Hodge, and Benjamin B. Warfield at Princeton; Kant through his influence on Friedrich

---

6. For a particularly enlightening account, see Stephen Toulmin, *Cosmopolis: The Hidden Agenda of Modernity* (New York: The Free Press, 1990). Other books that discuss or assume such a change are too numerous to list.

Schleiermacher and other nineteenth-century liberal theologians in Germany.[7] More about each of these in due course.

LIBERAL AND CONSERVATIVE THEOLOGIES

Scholars find it helpful to construct "ideal types," that is, constructs that distill out of the multiplicity of historical positions, configurations of ideas that fit together and characterize, to a greater or lesser degree, the members of a school or tradition. The German sociologist Max Weber (1864-1920) made great use of ideal types. His goal was to construct models of what economic agents would do if they were to act completely rationally. My goal is similar: to show that given the constraints of the modern philosophical worldview, there are two sets of theological moves that form a rational or consistent approach to theology.

While I cannot provide exhaustive historical evidence for this, I also claim that these two "packages" of theological moves can be related to the actual history of theology, especially in modern American Protestantism, and this accounts to a great extent for the differences between theologians we call liberal and those we call fundamentalist or evangelical.[8] It would be most interesting if I could show that theologians who tried to combine moves from both packages were judged by others to be unsuccessful.

Historian Claude Welch lists the following as characteristic elements of the mainstream of liberal theology:

the emphasis on divine immanence as a corrective to the Latin over-emphasis on transcendence . . . , thus a different view of God's relation

---

7. Cf. Nicholas Wolterstorff, "Tradition, Insight and Constraint," *Proceedings and Addresses of the American Philosophical Association* 66, no. 3 (November 1992): 43-57. "After Hume, the story branches, one leading to Thomas Reid, the other to Immanuel Kant. . . . The alternatives they develop are structurally identical, viz., elaborate and imaginative theories of the constraints of our constitution" (52).

8. The exact reference of these terms is a matter of contention. My take on the proper use of *liberal* and *conservative* will be the business of the first three chapters, so I shall not attempt to define these labels here. The fundamentalist movement in the United States can be defined as that which arose in the early twentieth century, stimulated by pamphlets called "The Fundamentals," emphasizing Calvinist orthodoxy along with scriptural inerrancy, substitutionary atonement, and the historicity of miracles, including the virgin birth of Christ. Evangelicals are sometimes called neo-fundamentalists, because many are former fundamentalists who have moderated their positions. However, the evangelical movement includes a broader range of Christians, such as Mennonites and Pentecostals, who intend to hold a middle position between fundamentalism and liberalism.

to the natural and historical process and an evolutionary perspective; the understanding of revelation not as an intrusion but as correlative to human discovery, as a process of God disclosing himself through genuine human means in a never-ending process of criticism and experiment; religious experience as a verifiable datum comparable to scientific data; the Bible as a document of religious experience and thus a different sort of authority.[9]

If we take the foregoing as an account of the liberal *type* of theology, we might construct a parallel account of conservative theology, both fundamentalist and conservative evangelical. First, in place of an emphasis on God's immanence there is a focus on God's power to intervene in natural and human affairs. Second, revelation itself is an intervention into human life; this revelation allows conservatives to maintain that the Scriptures do in fact convey information about God and God's relation to the universe. So, third, it is the Bible, not experience, that functions as the foundation (data) for theology. Finally, the emphasis on revelation as a source of information about divine realities hints at the conservatives' representative theory of religious language.

The task of the next three chapters is to explain each of these characteristics, showing how they fit into two consistent "packages," and in particular to show what modern philosophy had to do with making these options, and only these, available to the theologian.

It is important to reiterate that the goal of this study is to construct ideal types, not to write a history of modern theology. Therefore, no attempt will be made to provide an exhaustive survey of theologians, and it will not defeat my project if there are exceptions to the categories here described. The project, of course, would be entirely uninteresting if *no* modern theologians clearly fit the types. Thus, the views of representative theologians will be presented, both to illustrate the points being made and to show that the types are in fact embodied in history. The general plan is to refer regularly to the writings of two contemporary liberals (Gordon Kaufman and David Tracy); two contemporary conservatives (Donald Bloesch and Alister McGrath); and two each from a generation to a century ago (liberal: Harry Emerson Fosdick and Shailer Mathews; conservative: Charles Hodge and Augustus H. Strong). Two other characters make regular appearances due to their status as founders of traditions: Friedrich Schleiermacher, the founder of modern liberalism; and John Locke, known more as a philosopher than a theologian, but the one who gave modern conservative theology its rational structure. Others will be mentioned occasionally when they provide particularly apt illustrations of a point.

---

9. Claude Welch, *Protestant Thought in the Nineteenth Century*, 2 vols. (New Haven: Yale University Press, 1972, 1985), 2:232.

Part I

Experience or Scripture

How Do We Know God?

INTRODUCTION

It was a fateful day for modern Christians when the philosopher René Descartes was kept indoors by a cold spell in Germany. He seems to have divided his attention between a survey of the architecture he could observe from his window and a survey of the ideas in his mind, which he could observe by means of introspection. It was here, apparently, that the metaphor of knowledge as a building first gripped the philosophical imagination. Here is the comparison in Descartes's own words:

> We never tear down all the houses in a city just to rebuild them in a different way and to make the streets more beautiful; but we do see that individual owners often have theirs torn down and rebuilt, and even that they may be forced to do so when the building is crumbling with age, or when the foundation is not firm and it is in danger of collapsing. By this example I was convinced that . . . as far as the opinions which I had been receiving since my birth were concerned, I could not do better than to reject them completely for once in my lifetime, and to resume them afterwards, or perhaps accept better ones in their place, when I had determined how they fitted into a rational scheme. And I firmly believed that by this means I would succeed in conducting my life much better than if I built only upon the old foundations and gave credence to the principles which I had acquired in my childhood without ever having examined them to see whether they were true or not.[1]

---

1. René Descartes, *Discourse on Method* (1637), second part.

Notice the imagery. A system of knowledge is like a building, whose soundness depends on its foundation. If the foundation is not solid, it may need to be torn down and rebuilt on a new and stronger foundation. Philosophers are just now coming to recognize how influential this metaphor has been throughout the modern period—both in explicit "foundationalist" theories of knowledge and in everyday life. If readers who are not philosophers believe they have not been affected by this view, I suggest they consider how we talk about knowledge. Scientific knowledge is *based on* the facts; suspicions are *unfounded* or *groundless* or *baseless;* good arguments are *well-constructed* and *solid.*

The thesis of this chapter is that foundationalism has had a powerful influence on the development of modern theology. Theologians have conceived of theology as a building needing a sturdy foundation. But what is that foundation to be? The short answer is that there are only two options: Scripture and experience.[2] Conservative theologians have chosen to build upon Scripture; liberals are distinguished by their preference for experience. This forced option has been one cause of the split between liberals and conservatives.

DESCARTES'S FOUNDATIONALISM

Let us return now to Descartes. When Descartes set out to examine all of his inherited beliefs and to rebuild the system on a new foundation, he called into question the content of his knowledge. But at the same time he questioned medieval assumptions about the very nature of knowledge, rejecting the role of traditional authority—the *authority* of the *author*—and replacing it with the modern notion of indubitable beliefs *available to each individual.* This new conception became the dominant assumption of the modern period and set the conditions for all other intellectual work.[3]

So far I have spoken of foundationalism as a metaphor, but we are now able to put it in terms of a philosophical theory about knowledge. Specifically, it is a theory about how knowledge claims can be justified. When we seek to justify a belief, we do so by relating it to (basing it upon, deriving it from) other beliefs. If these other beliefs are called into question, then they too must be justified. Foundationalists insist that this chain of justifications must stop somewhere; it must not be circular or constitute an infinite re-

---

2. A longer answer would have to take into account the Catholic option of church teaching, and we shall see below that historical facts have figured into the account as well.

3. See Jeffrey Stout, *The Flight from Authority: Religion, Morality, and the Quest for Autonomy* (Notre Dame: University of Notre Dame Press, 1981).

gress. Thus, the regress must end in a "foundation" of beliefs that cannot themselves be called into question.[4]

Stephen Toulmin proposes an interesting explanation of Descartes's quest for certain foundations. In *Cosmopolis: The Hidden Agenda of Modernity*, he answers the question why the foundationalist theory appealed to Descartes and his followers at that particular point in intellectual history. Toulmin notes the coincidence of Descartes's life with the Thirty Years War. The bloodshed and chaos that followed upon seventeenth-century differences of belief lent urgency to the quest for universal agreement; the epistemologist could render a service to humanity by finding a way to produce such agreement. Science and religion stood for two paths to knowledge: pure reason versus traditional authority. If human reason was a faculty shared universally, then a new structure built on the deliverances of human reason must garner universal assent. So, from Descartes's time, the ideal of human knowledge focused on the general, the universal, the timeless, the theoretical—in contrast to the local, the particular, the timely, the practical.[5] In short, it is the quest for *universal* knowledge that drives the modern quest for *indubitable* foundations.

It is only recently that philosophers have labeled the modern foundationalist theory of knowledge as such,[6] so it is a view of knowledge that has merely been assumed by modern theologians, not explicitly advocated between the covers of their books. Thus, we will need a criterion by which to judge whether a thinker is a foundationalist or not. The use of foundationalist metaphors will provide clues, but the criteria I suggest are two: first, the assumption that knowledge systems must include a class of beliefs that are somehow immune from challenge; and, second, the assumption that all reasoning within the system proceeds in one direction only—from that set of special, indubitable beliefs to others, but not the reverse.

FOUNDATIONALISM IN EARLY MODERN PHILOSOPHY OF RELIGION

Let us now see how foundationalism shows up in early modern philosophy of religion. An interesting change from Descartes to John Locke concerns

---

4. For additional details, see Richard Rorty, *Philosophy and the Mirror of Nature* (Princeton, NJ: Princeton University Press, 1979), 157-63; Stout, *The Flight from Authority*, 3-5; Ronald Thiemann, *Revelation and Theology* (Notre Dame: University of Notre Dame Press, 1984), 44-46; and John E. Thiel, *Nonfoundationalism* (Minneapolis: Fortress Press, 1991).

5. Toulmin, *Cosmopolis*, chap. 1.

6. A rough indication here is that there is no entry for foundationalism in the Collier-Macmillan *Encyclopedia of Philosophy*, published in 1967.

the question whether religious knowledge is part of one great structure that includes knowledge of the empirical world as well, or whether religious knowledge forms a separate edifice. Descartes argued from the "clear and distinct ideas" in his mind (such as *I am thinking)* to the existence of God, and from there to knowledge of the external world. So he envisioned the whole of knowledge as one great building, founded on special, indubitable ideas, with theological knowledge sandwiched in between these ideas and science.

The British empiricist John Locke was much influenced by Descartes, but he distinguished three kinds of knowledge: There was empirical science, founded on ideas from sensory experience. There was also Descartes's notion of indubitable knowledge, based on ideas and constructed by means of deductive reasoning; geometry is one instance of this, and another is Locke's argument for the existence of God.[7] There was yet a third kind of knowledge based on revelation, that is, on God's "extraordinary way of communication." In *The Reasonableness of Christianity,* published in 1695, Locke presented his conclusions regarding the theological doctrines that could be certified on the basis of scriptural revelation. The messiahship of Jesus was essential, but some doctrines, such as the Trinity and predestination, he judged unfounded.

So we may imagine the epistemological scene as envisioned by Locke to include the great edifice of science, a separate structure of theology founded upon Scripture, and additional deductive structures founded upon "the relations of ideas." But the theological structure is not entirely independent of the deductive argument for the existence of God; God's existence makes the whole idea of revelation intelligible. So I like to fancy these last two structures as connected by an arch or buttress.

The problem Locke faced, and one that has plagued scriptural foundationalists ever since, is how to know that *this* book, the Christian Bible, is in fact the expected revelation. The very fact that this question can be asked creates problems for a foundationalist use of Scripture—it undermines it. Conservative apologetics from Locke's day to the present have attempted to shore up the basement. Locke argued that miracles served as outward signs to convince "the holy men of old" that God was indeed the author of their purported revelations:

> Thus we see the holy men of old, who had *revelations* from God, had something else besides that internal light of assurance in their own minds to testify to them that it was from God. They were not left to their own persuasions alone that those persuasions were from God, but had outward signs to convince them of the author of those revela-

---

7. John Locke, *An Essay concerning Human Understanding* (New York: Dover, 1959). First published in 1690.

tions. And when they were to convince others, they had a power given them to justify the truth of their commission from heaven, and by visible signs to assert the divine authority of a message they were sent with.[8]

Another standard argument has been to point to the prophecies in Scripture and to argue that their fulfillment shows that the knowledge is supernatural and therefore from God.

FOUNDATIONALISM IN CONSERVATIVE THEOLOGY

We shall presently take up the criticisms that led liberal theologians to abandon Locke's theological structure, but first it will be interesting to see how it has continued to influence conservative theologians, especially in America. Great impetus came from the philosophical writings of Thomas Reid, founder of the school of philosophy called common-sense realism. Reid influenced Princeton theologians such as Charles Hodge (1797-1878) and Charles's son, Archibald Alexander Hodge (1823-86), whose work, in turn, greatly influenced the American fundamentalist movement. Reid's role, as we shall see below, was to call into question the philosophical arguments that had been taken by liberals to undermine Locke's apologetic structure.

A fine example of Locke's pattern of argument is found in the writings of Augustus H. Strong (1836-1921), a Baptist, whose systematic theology was first published in 1876.[9] For Strong, theology is the science of God and of the relation between God and the universe (1) and not, he insists, the science of the Christian religion. Its aim is to ascertain the facts respecting God and to exhibit these facts in an organic system of truth. The possibility of theology is grounded in the existence of God and in God's self-revelation. Revelation presents "objective facts," which serve as "the ground of theology" (13). Systematic theology "takes the material furnished by Biblical and Historical Theology and with this material seeks to build up into an organic and consistent whole all our knowledge of God and of the relations between God and the universe" (41). Note the foundationalist metaphors: facts from Scripture as ground, theology as building. The foundationalist picture is even clearer in the following reply to critics:

Hume and Gibbon refer to faith as something too sacred to rest on proof. Thus religious beliefs are made to hang in mid-air, without any

---

8. Locke, *Essay*, IV, xix, 15.

9. Augustus H. Strong, *Systematic Theology: A Compendium and Commonplace-Book*, enl. ed. (Philadelphia: Judson Press, 1907). Page numbers in parentheses refer to the twelfth edition, 1949.

support. But the foundation of these beliefs is no less solid for the reason that empirical tests are not applicable to them. The data on which they rest are real, and the inferences from the data are fairly drawn (15).

Later sections of the book offer Cartesian and Lockean-style proofs for the existence of God (71-89), "reasons *a priori* for expecting a revelation from God" (111-14), and "positive proofs that the Scriptures are a divine revelation" (145-95).

The special foundational status of Scripture is also well represented in the following quotation from Charles Hodge, in which he claims that even if there are other sources of theological knowledge, each must be tested against the biblical norm:

> The duty of the Christian theologian is to ascertain, collect, and com-bine all the facts which God has revealed in the Bible. . . . It may be admitted that the truths which the theologian has to reduce to a sci-ence, or, to speak more humbly, which he has to arrange and harmo-nize, are revealed partly in the external works of God, partly in the constitution of our nature, and partly in the religious experience of believers; yet lest we should err in our inferences from the works of God, we have a clearer revelation of all that nature reveals, in his word; and lest we should misinterpret our own consciousness and the laws of our nature, everything that can be legitimately learned from that source will be found recognized and authenticated in the Scrip-tures; and lest we should attribute to the teaching of the Spirit the operations of our own natural affections, we find in the Bible the norm and standard of all genuine religious experience.[10]

From the perspective of the epistemologist, an interesting feature of fun-damentalist and conservative evangelical theology is the sort of claims that are made about Scripture. One of the central tenets of fundamentalism is the verbal inspiration of Scripture and its complete inerrancy. It is claimed by some critics of the inerrantists that strict doctrines of inerrancy did not appear in Christian history until the modern period.[11] Conservatives who hold the doctrine, however, claim that it has been the traditional under-standing of the nature of Scripture. Notice that foundationalist epistemol-ogy explains why conservatives would *want* to be able to make such radical

---

10. Charles Hodge, *Systematic Theology*, 3 vols. (New York: Scribner's Sons, 1891), 1:11. First edition, 1871.

11. A. A. Hodge made explicit the Princeton doctrine of plenary verbal inspira-tion, claiming that the Bible is inerrant in its original autographs and infallible in what it teaches. See Hodge, *Outlines of Theology* (1878) and "Inspiration," *Pres-byterian Review* (1881), written with Benjamin B. Warfield.

claims about the truth of Scripture[12]: if Scripture is to provide an *indubitable* foundation for theological construction, then all of its teachings must be free from error, lest the theologian make erroneous judgments in distinguishing true teachings from false ones or essential teachings from incidental cultural assumptions. Not all conservative theologians are infallibilists or inerrantists, but we can see that the *ideal type* of scriptural foundationalist theology would be expected to have such a doctrine.

Early conservative theologians vary in their accounts of the means of construction from Scripture to theology. They tend to speak rather indiscriminately of induction, of deduction, and of theology as mere organization of the facts of Scripture. But in all cases the assumed direction of reasoning is what the foundationalist theory would lead us to expect: from the scriptural foundation to the higher levels of doctrine and theology, never from doctrine to the truth or meaning of the texts.

Among contemporary conservatives we find more nuanced accounts of the foundational role of Scripture in theology. Donald Bloesch, emeritus professor of theology at Dubuque Theological Seminary, is explicitly foundationalist in his understanding of the justification of theological claims:

> As evangelical Christians we can and must speak of *foundations* of the faith. These are not, however, a priori principles or self-evident truths but the mighty deeds of God in the history of biblical Israel, the significance of which is veiled to us until our inner eyes are opened by the working of the Spirit.[13]

So, in contrast to the view of such as A. A. Hodge, it is not the words of Scripture themselves that undergird theology, but rather the acts of God that are recorded therein. Furthermore, Bloesch distinguishes between purely historical events and their "revelational meaning" (19). To illustrate: one can believe that Jesus' tomb was empty and even that he rose from the dead without grasping the revelation that Jesus is the divine savior of the world.

Bloesch would like to be able to say that the Scriptures are inerrant, but he believes the term has been coopted by "a rationalistic, empiricistic mentality that reduces faith to facticity" (27). Instead, he speaks of the abiding truthfulness and normativeness of the biblical witness (27). "What makes the Bible significant is not that it contains self-evident truth—truth that is universally recognizable—but that it conveys particular truth that is at the same time self-authenticating" (28).

So we see here a softening of the original foundationalist demand for *universally* accessible truth based on *indubitable* foundations. Yet despite

---

12. And why the doctrine should emerge in its present form only in the modern period, if, in fact, this is the case.

13. Donald G. Bloesch, *Holy Scripture: Revelation, Inspiration and Interpretation* (Downers Grove, IL: InterVarsity Press, 1994), 20.

the hesitancy regarding inerrancy (and the absolute certitude such a doctrine provides), it is still the case that the authority of Scripture is *unchallengeable.* There is no other norm by which it can be called into question, neither religious experience, nor church teaching, nor culture.[14]

Alister McGrath, lecturer at Wycliff Hall, Oxford, also speaks of theology in foundationalist terms and gives biblical revelation an unchallenged role in theology. In his textbook for university students he puts it simply:

> The ultimate source of Christian theology is the Bible, which bears witness to the historical grounding of Christianity in both the history of Israel and the life, death, and resurrection of Jesus Christ.[15]

In a more technical work, McGrath emphasizes the narrative form of the biblical witness:

> The narrative of Jesus Christ, mediated through scripture and eucharistic celebration, is presented, proclaimed *and accepted* as the foundational and controlling narrative of the community of faith.
>
> This narrative is transmitted through scripture, or channels which may be shown to be directly derived from this source. The primary source of Christian doctrine is thus scripture.[16]

Doctrine provides a conceptual structure by which the scriptural narrative is interpreted. McGrath recognizes that doctrinal formulations can lead us to reread the narrative in a different light, and so there is a sense of two-way interchange between the foundation and the superstructure. Thus, we can see that McGrath is chafing against the foundationalist model, even while he uses especially vivid foundationalist imagery in describing the relation between the scriptural narrative and the doctrinal superstructure:

> The transition from a narrative to a conceptual framework of thinking would have potentially destructive effects for Christian theology if the narrative concerning Jesus of Nazareth, having been allowed to generate a specific framework of conceptualities, were forgotten. Had a conceptual approach to Christianity (such as that associated with the concept of incarnation) been regarded as self-sufficient and autonomous, the narrative which originally precipitated it might have disap-

---

14. See Donald G. Bloesch, *Essentials of Evangelical Theology, Volume 1: God, Authority, and Salvation* (San Francisco: Harper & Row, 1978), chap. 4.

15. Alister E. McGrath, *Christian Theology: An Introduction* (Oxford: Blackwell, 1994), 119.

16. Alister E. McGrath, *The Genesis of Doctrine: A Study in the Foundations of Doctrinal Criticism* (Oxford: Basil Blackwell, 1990), 55.

peared into the mists of history. Had this occurred, serious anxiety would necessarily have resulted concerning the propriety and adequacy of this framework. It would have been left suspended without visible support. No criteria, save those imposed from outside by rival ideologies, could be adduced by which it could be evaluated. However, the foundational narrative has been preserved by the community of faith, and accorded primary status in doctrinal reflection (64).

We might call McGrath a narrative foundationalist rather than a scriptural foundationalist.

UNDERMINING LOCKE

Let us now retrace our path, noting the factors that drove liberal theologians to abandon the structure of religious knowledge first set out by John Locke. Recall that I described Locke's view of religious knowledge rather whimsically as two structures connected by a buttress: theology is founded upon Scripture, but Scripture's authority derives from the fact that it is revealed by God. One of the ways in which the claim for revelation is buttressed is by means of a rational argument for the existence of God and the further inference that such a God must be expected to reveal himself. The Scriptures are then shown by various arguments to be that expected revelation.

Two factors conspired to demolish the confidence of many theologians in the Lockean structure. One was the work of philosophers such as David Hume in Britain and Immanuel Kant in Germany, showing that traditional arguments for the existence of God are invalid. By Hume's day the most important arguments were design arguments, based on the premises that the universe is like a complex machine or mechanism and that all complex mechanisms have to have designers. One of Hume's attacks on this argument consisted in pointing out that the hypothesis of an intelligent designer is only one possible explanation of the origin of the universe and depends on our first construing it as a machine or mechanism. If we construe it instead as more analogous to an organism, then it could be produced by propagation. A more telling argument for today was his suggestion that, since we have no experience at all of the origin of universes in general, for all we know it could be the result of a fortuitous arrangement of atoms.[17]

The other factor had to do with shifting views of the proper relation between reason and revelation. For Locke, if reason could show that a particular book was the product of divine revelation, then it was reasonable to

---

17. David Hume, *Dialogues concerning Natural Religion*, probably written in the 1750s but first published posthumously in 1779.

accept all of its contents even if the contents themselves could not be certified as true on the basis of reason. Locke had written:

> *Reason* must be our last judge and guide in everything. I do not mean
> that we must consult reason and examine whether a proposition re-
> vealed from God can be made out by natural principles, and if it can-
> not, that then we may reject it; but consult it we must, and by it exam-
> ine whether it be a revelation from God or no; and if *reason* finds it to
> be revealed from God, *reason* then declares for it as much as for any
> other truth, and makes it one of her dictates.[18]

The eighteenth-century British Deists granted reason a more significant
role, saying that only those tenets of traditional theology that can be established by reason *independently* of revelation ought to be accepted. Thus,
reasonableness became a criterion for what is or is not to be accepted within
the scriptural accounts.

Hume went even further in his attack, arguing that we can never have
enough reason to believe that a miracle has taken place so as to use it to
support a system of religion. He undercut Locke's apologetic strategy of
basing the revelatory status of the Scriptures on miracles.

> Upon the whole, then, it appears, that no testimony for any kind of
> miracle has ever amounted to a probability, much less to a proof; and
> that, even supposing it amounted to a proof, it would be opposed by
> another proof; derived from the very nature of the fact, which it would
> endeavour to establish. It is experience only, which gives authority to
> human testimony; and it is the same experience, which assures us of
> the laws of nature. When, therefore, these two kinds of experience are
> contrary, we have nothing to do but subtract the one from the other,
> and embrace an opinion, either on one side or the other, with that
> assurance which arises from the remainder. But according to the prin-
> ciple here explained, this subtraction, with regard to all popular reli-
> gions, amounts to an entire annihilation; and therefore we may estab-
> lish it as a maxim, that no human testimony can have such force as to
> prove a miracle, and make it a just foundation for any such system of
> religion.[19]

In this passage Hume is arguing that the fact that a miracle is a violation of
the laws of nature puts any claim to have witnessed a miracle in competition
with our knowledge of the regularities of nature. This makes it far less cred-
ible than testimonies that agree with experiential knowledge. He is not ar-

---

18. Locke, *Essay,* IV, xix, 14. See also IV, xvi, 14.
19. David Hume, "Of Miracles," in *Enquiry concerning Human Understanding*
(1748), part II.

guing that miracles cannot happen, but only that we can never have enough evidence, all things considered, to believe one has occurred—and especially not enough to make miracles the ultimate foundation for an entire structure of religious beliefs. With this argument Hume has now undermined both sides of Locke's theological and apologetic structure—the side based on arguments for the existence of God as well as the side based on Scripture attested by miracles.

In eighteenth-century Germany there had been a move similar to Locke's to shore up orthodox forms of belief by seeking rational support for the claims of revelation. Then, in a manner exactly parallel to the Deists, the neologists restricted the content of divine revelation to what can be known independently by natural reason.[20] Thus, reason was unleashed to sift the Scriptures for truth, and in subsequent generations many concluded that what remained after the sifting was too little to support the structure of orthodox Christian theology.

The most significant program for sifting Scripture's truth-claims was the application of historical-critical methods to the Bible. Results of study of the Old Testament ranged from modest conclusions about dating and authorship to outright rejection of the historicity of most of the texts. Historical criticism of the New Testament focused on attempts to reconstruct the life of Jesus. In the eighteenth century suspicion arose that the texts were misrepresenting the teaching of Jesus, and it was hoped that historical-critical methods could uncover the real history behind the texts. The quest began with an anonymous publication (in 1778) by H. S. Reimarus, who portrayed Jesus as a messianic leader more nationalistic than religious. Later contributions varied widely from extreme skepticism to confident endorsement of the Gospels' portrayals.

The most significant figure in bringing the nineteenth-century quest to an end was Albert Schweitzer (1875-1965). Schweitzer well expresses the liberals' conclusion that what historical reason leaves standing is too meager a foundation for Christianity, and in the following passage he describes the crucial shift from Scripture construed as a source of historical knowledge to ongoing religious experience as foundational for Christianity.

The historical foundation of Christianity as built up by rationalistic, by liberal, and by modern theology no longer exists; but that does not mean that Christianity has lost its historical foundation. The work which historical theology thought itself bound to carry out, and which fell to pieces just as it was nearing completion, was only the brick facing of the real immovable historical foundation which is independent of any historical confirmation or justification.

---

20. See Richard Crouter, "Introduction," in Friedrich Schleiermacher, *On Religion: Speeches to Its Cultured Despisers* (Cambridge: Cambridge University Press, 1988), 6-7.

Jesus means something to our world because a mighty spiritual force streams forth from Him and flows through our time also. This fact can neither be shaken nor confirmed by any historical discovery. It is the solid foundation of Christianity.[21]

So reason, once the buttress supporting a theology founded on scriptural revelation, has now undermined the structure. If Scripture is to serve at all, it must be a repository of something more basic, less prone to rationalist attack. That more basic something—for Schweitzer, the mighty spiritual force streaming from Jesus through our own time—can be categorized more broadly as religious experience.

FOUNDATIONALISM IN MODERN LIBERAL THEOLOGY

With Schweitzer, writing in 1906, we have gotten ahead of our story. Let us go back now to the beginning of modern liberal theology. In 1799 Friedrich Schleiermacher (1768-1834) published his famous *Speeches,* in which he put forward the view that the essence of religion (of all religion, not just Christianity) is a certain sort of feeling or awareness. He described this feeling differently over the years of his theological career: as "intuition of the infinite," as "immediate perception of the universe and of the existence of all finite things in and through the infinite," as "immediate consciousness of the deity," and finally in his mature work as "awareness of absolute dependence," or, what he took to be the same, as "God consciousness."

Schleiermacher's achievement in the systematic theology of his later years was to show that all legitimate doctrines were derivable from this foundational experience. But they were not derivable in a logical sense, but rather in the sense that they were apt or adequate *expressions* of that core experience. So, for example, the source of the doctrine of creation is the awareness not only of our own dependence upon God but of the absolute dependence of everything else as well. The doctrines of sin and grace express our experience of the waxing and waning of our God-consciousness. The divinity of Christ consists in his uninterrupted and perfect God-consciousness.

Now, in what sense is this a foundationalist use of experience for theology? Recall the criteria I set out earlier: First, the experience has to be unchallengeable. For Schleiermacher's purposes this means it must be universal and unmediated. It is universal in the sense that while it is colored differently in different cultures—and for Christians, especially, by the influence of Jesus—it is the common source of *all* religions. It is a kind of experience that is available in principle to all human beings, not just Christians.

---

21. Albert Schweitzer, *The Quest of the Historical Jesus* (New York: Macmillan, 1950), 399. Written in 1906.

When Schleiermacher claims that the awareness of absolute dependence is unmediated he means that it is not dependent upon inference or interpretation. It is the true source or origin of religion, not a product of anything prior. In other words, there is no deeper foundation.

The second criterion for foundationalist epistemology is one-way reasoning. This requirement is satisfied in Schleiermacher's system in that doctrine is to be evaluated in light of experience, never the reverse. So God-consciousness is the foundation of all religion; first-order religious language (prayer, preaching, and so forth), as well as doctrine and theology, are all built up from this experience. Liberal theologians since Schleiermacher have followed him in taking human religious experience or awareness as a universal feature of human life and in supposing that this religious self-consciousness was to be the starting point for theology.

In America the early-twentieth-century modernists offered experiential accounts of Christian theology. For example, Shailer Mathews (1863-1941), professor of theology at the University of Chicago, emphasized the priority of religion over doctrine. Religion itself is a matter of experience, attitudes, and moral convictions. Christian doctrines are verbal expressions of the religious life, making use of patterns of thought current in each era of Christian history. They are to be judged on the basis of their effectiveness in inspiring religious convictions and loyalties.[22]

The noted Baptist pastor and preacher Harry Emerson Fosdick (1878-1969) spoke instead of doctrines "springing from" and "expressing" the religious life.

All doctrines spring from life. In the first instance men have experiences with their own souls, with their fellows, with their God, which, involving mental elements as all sane experiences must, are nevertheless primarily valued for their contribution to the practical richness of life. Unable, however, to deny their intellectual necessities, men carry these experiences up into their minds and try deliberately to explain, unify, organize, and rationalize them. They make systematized doctrines out of their experiences. And when the formula has been constructed, they love it because the experience for which it stands is precious.

However, when new ways of thinking develop, the old formulas become unintelligible and produce conflict.

The way out leads inevitably through liberalism. Some . . . discover that their religion does not consist in the formula but in the experience of which the formula is a transient phrasing. They become liberals by

---

22. Shailer Mathews, *The Faith of Modernism* (New York: Macmillan, 1924). This is said to have been liberalism's most widely read book in the 1920s.

retreating from the formula into the experience behind it, by translating the formula back into the life out of which it came.[23]

Notice that these liberals do not deny a role for Scripture in theology; they merely deny that it is the foundation for theology. That is, Scripture itself is undergirded by a theory of universal religious experience. So one might say that experience is the foundation and Scripture is the ground floor.

Mathews emphasizes that the Bible is a progressive record of religious experience in its historical development. "The Bible when properly arranged on the basis of satisfactory [historical-critical] evidence is a trustworthy record of human experience of God."[24] And, as for Schweitzer and Fosdick, the important thing is not the past experience itself, but its continuation into the present:

> Christianity becomes not the acceptance of a literature but a reproduction of attitudes and faith, a fellowship with those ancient men of imperfect morals whose hearts found God, whose lives were strengthened by the divine spirit, whose words point out the way of life, and who determined the inner character of the Christian religion. From such sources the major doctrines are derived. Other elements are secondary accretions from contemporary religions, easily and repeatedly separated from the religion of Jesus Christ.[25]

When we reach the contemporary period, we find accounts of theology that are extremely subtle and complex. In fact, it has become common to find entire tomes dedicated to explication of theological method. Our examples here will be David Tracy, a Catholic professor of theology at the University of Chicago Divinity School,[26] and Gordon Kaufman, a professor (with a Mennonite background) at Harvard Divinity School.

It is clear that both Tracy and Kaufman are dissatisfied with the modern dichotomy between Scripture and experience as sources for theology, yet both ultimately give priority to experience. They also chafe against the limits of the foundationalist model of knowledge and, in some instances, speak in ways that suggest they have transcended it. Yet no coherent epistemological model is offered to replace the foundationalist model,[27] and I believe that

---

23. Harry Emerson Fosdick, *The Modern Use of the Bible* (London: SCM, 1924), 185-86.

24. Mathews, *The Faith of Modernism*, 47.

25. Ibid., 49-50.

26. It may seem odd to include this one Catholic as an illustration; I do so because of his stature in contemporary theology and also because his Catholic heritage seems to make no difference to his theological method.

27. I may be misjudging Kaufman here; he claims to develop a holist theological model in *In Face of Mystery: A Constructive Theology* (Cambridge, MA: Harvard University Press, 1993).

despite the reservations and qualifications it is fair to say that the basic structure of experiential foundationalism remains.

In his earlier methodological treatise, *Blessed Rage for Order,* Tracy describes himself (and Kaufman as well) as revisionist theologians. This approach holds that "a contemporary fundamental Christian theology can best be described as philosophical reflection upon the meanings present in common human experience and language and upon the meanings present in the Christian fact [or tradition; cf. page 34]."[28] This sounds like the rejection of experiential foundationalism in favor of an interaction between tradition and experience. Whether this is so, however, depends on what is meant by "the meanings present in the Christian fact/tradition," and on whether tradition and experience contribute equally to the resulting theology.

Tracy's answer to the last question is clear: the scriptural claim that Christian self-understanding expresses an understanding of authentic human existence is to be tested against the criterion of adequacy to common human experience (44).

In *The Analogical Imagination* Tracy develops the claim that the Christian Scriptures are best understood as literary classics, and the task of interpreting them is to be understood as an instance of the interpretation of any classic work of art. Tracy's commitment to an experiential approach to theology becomes even clearer in his claim that classics are expressions of an experience that he terms "an event of understanding."[29] The appreciation of a classic is itself an experience—"a realized experience of an event of truth" (111). The work of art produces an experience of shock, surprise, recognition, and in fact is judged to be a classic by its ability to produce such reactions again and again:

> It remains the realized experience which must serve as the first word and the final criterion of relative adequacy in any attempt at both understanding and explanation. For only a realized experience and its disclosure of some recognition of the event-character of truth in the work of art will finally count for each as evidence (113).

The role of Scripture, then, is that the Christian classic texts preserve the memory of Jesus of Nazareth, which serves to focus contemporary experiences of the Christ event. It is this experience that is to be correlated with (tested against) the meanings found within common human experience.

Kaufman begins *An Essay on Theological Method* with an expression of dissatisfaction with the foundationalist options for theology. In light of the

---

28. David Tracy, *Blessed Rage for Order: The New Pluralism in Theology* (New York: Seabury Press, 1978), 43.

29. David Tracy, *The Analogical Imagination: Christian Theology and the Culture of Pluralism* (New York: Crossroad, 1981), 102.

breakdown of the neo-orthodox view of the authority of God's revelation as the ultimate court of appeal for theology, Kaufman claims that he was forced "to attempt to think through afresh the task of theology and to search for new and more adequate foundations."[30] However, he finds it impossible simply to found theology on religious experience because of the problem of determining what counts as religious experience. Kaufman chooses instead to base theology on broader cultural experience (3). This experience is captured in common language, and thus

> it would be truer to say that the language we speak provides a principal foundation for our religious experience, than to hold that some pre-conceptual, pre-linguistic raw experience is the principal foundation of our theological language and thought (6).

Theology, then, is conceptual clarification of the religious terms found in ordinary language. Kaufman's particular concern is with the concept *God,* which, following Kant, he understands as a regulative concept, constructed to make sense of a set of concepts drawn from experience.

So in both cases we find an emphasis on experience—the religious dimension of common human experience, or linguistic expressions based on cultural experience—as the final court of appeal for theology. The earlier foundationalist emphasis on certitude has been replaced with a concern for the "publicness" of the criteria for judging theology, but this "new" quest for public consensus, if Toulmin's analysis is correct, is the same as that which drove the seventeenth-century development of the foundationalist epistemological theory in the first place.

I now want to reflect on two general features of liberal theologies that may strike the uninitiated as peculiar. The first is the attempt to understand Christianity by setting it within the context of world religions, in contrast to the more traditional attempts to understand other religions in light of Christian convictions. The second, related feature is the peculiar *nature* of the experiences cited as foundational for Christian theology. There is, for example, Schleiermacher's feeling of absolute dependence. "Feeling" here translates the German word *Gefühl,* but it is not an adequate translation. In attempting to convey the sort of experience that is meant, Claude Welch writes:

> *Gefühl* is not a "faculty" parallel to the faculties of thinking and willing. . . . Feeling was equated with immediate self-consciousness. The feeling of utter dependence belonged to the highest level of human self-consciousness, in which the antithesis between the self and other

---

30. Gordon Kaufman, *An Essay on Theological Method,* rev. ed. (Missoula, MT: Scholars Press, 1979), x.

which characterizes the sensuous self-consciousness disappears again.
. . . It is thus the deepest (or highest) level of self-existence, not an
isolable "religious experience," but an "original relation of intuition
and feeling."[31]

Many Christians might well wonder if they have ever had such an experience!

Other liberal theologians provide equally abstruse accounts of foundational religious experience. Tracy's may be the winner here. In *Blessed Rage for Order* he speaks of "limit experiences" as disclosing the religious dimension of common human experience. For example, "All genuine limit-situations refer to those experiences, both positive and negative, wherein we both experience our own human limits (limit-to) as our own as well as recognize, however haltingly, some disclosure of a limit-of our experience" (105). In *The Analogical Imagination* his emphasis shifts to the aesthetic experience involved in the appreciation of a classic, of which religious experience is an instance.

> In experiencing a classic I recognize a truth I somehow know but know I did not really know except through the experience of recognition of the essential compelled by the work of art. . . . I do not experience a subject over against an object with my subjective consciousness in complete control. Rather I experience myself caught up in a relationship with the work of art in such a manner that I transcend my everyday self-consciousness. . . . I experience the impact of a realized experience, an event character of truth as a glimpse into the essential that is real (111-12).

The question then may arise: why such accounts as these in place of what the plain speaker of English might mean by "religious experience"—narrative accounts of experiences in prayer, or conversion, and so forth? The foundationalist theory answers this question, as well as the question why liberal theologians treat Christianity as but an instance of the broader category of *religion:* Foundations must be *universal* and *immune from challenge*. Therefore, the requisite experiences must not be specifically Christian in character, nor subject to mistake or misinterpretation, as accounts of "what happened" always are—there are spurious conversions, imagined answers in prayer.

So a thoroughgoing experiential foundationalist must base the system on a kind of experience that is available to *all* people, regardless of culture and religious training, and it must be immediate, independent of interpretation, and such that one is unable to doubt that one has it or be mistaken about its

---

31. Welch, *Protestant Thought in the Nineteenth Century*, 1:66.

character. Not all theologians who count themselves in the liberal tradition will fit this ideal type, of course,[32] but one can see here a rationale for experiential foundationalists to seek an experience that moves as far in this direction as possible.

Let me sum up so far. I have claimed that a philosophical theory, characteristic of modern thought in general and derived from the metaphor of knowledge as a building, has had a dramatic effect on conceptions of the nature of theology. If theology must have a solid foundation, a natural direction to turn was to Scripture, and here one will be driven rationally toward an inerrantist account of its truth. I have also described some of the factors that led liberal theologians to seek a deeper level of support in religious experience and have claimed that the foundationalist theory led them, further, to seek for a peculiar sort of experience, universal and unmediated.

Thus, we see that there are two distinct strategies for satisfying the demand for indubitable foundations for theology. The Scriptures themselves are understood differently by proponents of the two strategies. Conservatives emphasize that these books are the result of acts of God, not of human discovery, and emphasize as well the factual character of their contents. The Scriptures provide precise and true accounts of supernatural realities. Liberals see the Christian Scriptures as belonging to a class of writings that express, with different degrees of aptitude, insights regarding God and human life that arise from religious experience. So, according to liberals, the Christian Scriptures may be especially authoritative for Christians, but they differ from other religious writings in degree, not in kind. Here the emphasis is on adequacy of expression or ability to engender religious experience rather than on factuality or precision or accurate representation of states of affairs.

INSIDE-OUT EPISTEMOLOGY

We have just considered the consequences of foundationalism for theologians' views of proper methods for theology. Here we consider another feature of the modern understanding of knowledge, shared by most modern philosophers, and trace its appearance in theology.

Wallace Matson points out that there have been two approaches in philosophy, from ancient times to the present, which he calls "outside-in" and "inside-out." Outside-in philosophy begins with an account of the world and later explains the human mind and its knowledge in terms developed in that account. Inside-out philosophy begins with the contents of the mind and then seeks to give an account of the world in those terms.[33]

---

32. Fosdick's and Mathews's accounts are closer to the common meaning of "religious experience."

33. Matson, *A New History of Philosophy*, 2:275-6.

Most but not all modern epistemologists have taken an inside-out approach to knowledge. Descartes made a sharp distinction between the mind and material reality. There were two kinds of substances, he claimed, one kind characterized by its extension in space, and the other non-spatial and characterized by its ability to think. The contents of thought, or of the mind, were ideas. The term *idea* refers to a variety of mental contents: pains, emotions, mental images, and thoughts such as *there must be at least as much reality in the efficient and total cause as in its effect.*

It is common now to speak of ideas being "in the mind," so this bit of philosophy has affected ordinary thinking about thinking. An aspect of modern inside-out epistemology that has not made its way into ordinary language is the view that knowledge of material objects is not based on our seeing them directly but is mediated by our inspection of mental representations. The reasoning that led philosophers to take this turn goes something like this: If I look at a square table from any position other than directly above, what I see is not square but trapezoidal. If what I see is trapezoidal and the table itself is square, then I must not be seeing the table itself; instead I see a representation, and that representation is "in my mind." This way of thinking about perceptual knowledge was reinforced by what scientists were learning about the physics of sensory perception; for instance, color sensations are produced in the brain by the eye's reception of light waves of different lengths.

The knowledge problem, then, is how to know that the mental ideas accurately represent external reality—or if indeed there is an external reality at all. Thus, typical modern accounts of knowledge involve two parts: first, an investigation of mental *contents;* second an *argument* of some sort to justify the claim that the mental contents give true and accurate knowledge of what is outside the mind. For example, Descartes argued that it would be deceptive for God to have constructed us with these sensory experiences if they were not generally accurate representations of the real world, and since it is incompatible with the *idea* of God (another of the contents of Descartes's mind) that God should be a deceiver, he was justified in believing that what he seemed to perceive did in fact exist.

One of Descartes's arguments for the existence of God has the same inside-out character. Part of his argument is the following:

There only remains, therefore, the idea of God, in which I must consider whether there is anything that cannot be supposed to originate with myself. By the name God, I understand a substance infinite, eternal, immutable, independent, all-knowing, all-powerful, and by which I myself, and every other thing that exists, if any such there be, were created. But these properties are so great and excellent, that the more attentively I consider them the less I feel persuaded that the idea I have of them owes its origin to myself alone. And thus it is absolutely necessary to conclude, from all that I have before said, that God exists: for though the idea of substance be in my mind owing to this, that I myself am a substance, I should not, however, have the idea of an infinite substance, seeing I am a finite being, unless it were given me by some substance in reality infinite.[34]

Here Descartes is considering whether or not the idea of God that he has found in his mind represents an existent being with the properties included in his idea. To answer the question he must determine what caused him to have that idea. Since "there must be as much reality in the efficient and total cause as in its effect," he concludes that only God is great enough (has enough reality) to have caused such an idea and, therefore, God must exist.

Descartes's argument for the existence of God is especially questionable by contemporary standards because it relies on medieval views about gradations and kinds of reality and their causal relations that have no counterpart today. However, once a wedge has been driven between directly accessible mental contents and external realities knowable only by means of those representations, there will always be worries about the arguments from inside to outside, from ideas to reality, because there is by definition no way to compare the idea with what it is supposed to represent—whether the idea is of God or of a table! This is one of the reasons that modern philosophy has been constantly obsessed with skepticism.

Given the predominance of inside-out approaches to philosophy in the modern period, it should come as no surprise to find inside-out theologies as well. This has been the regular pattern of the liberal tradition. It is said that the beginning of modern liberal theology is marked by the subjective turn, a "Copernican revolution," that places the human subject at the center of religion. Claude Welch writes:

In the work of Schleiermacher and [Samuel Taylor] Coleridge particularly . . . we see a decisive Socratic turn to the self, to an understanding of religious truth that may rightly be called "existentialist." Theology now had to start from, to articulate, and to interpret a subjective view of the religious object. . . . Consciousness of the truth was peculiarly one with self-consciousness.[35]

We have already noted above the peculiar character of the experiences that serve as the foundation for liberal theologies; their "inward" character is a part of this peculiarity. The following quotation from Schleiermacher reflects both his inside-out approach and his foundationalism. Regarding Christian beliefs he states: "There is an inner experience to which they may

---

34. René Descartes, *Meditations on First Philosophy* (1641), Third Meditation.
35. Welch, *Protestant Thought in the Nineteenth Century*, 1:59-60.

all be traced; they rest upon a given, and apart from this they could not have arisen by deduction or synthesis from universally recognized propositions."[36] So it is an *inner* experience that provides the foundation (a "given") for religious beliefs.

If inside-out approaches always invite the criticism that they have not adequately assured that the inner reflects the outer, we should not be surprised that already in 1841 Ludwig Feuerbach had charged that the idea of God is nothing more than an idea.[37] Feuerbach's theory of religion can be summarized as follows. The possibility of religion lies in consciousness, in the possibility of an inner life. The basis of religion is found in feelings or emotions and in wishes. "Man believes in gods because he seeks help from them. What he is not himself but wishes to be, he projects into the being of the gods in order that he may get it back from them."[38]

To put it in terms of our discussion of Descartes, whereas Descartes believed that only a real, objective God external to the believer was capable of producing the idea of God, Feuerbach argues that humans are quite capable of producing such an idea simply by summing up their own highest aspirations. So the argument from inner idea to external God fails. This led twentieth-century, neo-orthodox theologian Karl Barth to conclude that a starting point for theology like Schleiermacher's will lead inevitably to a skeptical conclusion like Feuerbach's.[39]

And so we should not be surprised, either, to find that the brief and simple accounts of the relation between religious experience and theology in Mathews and Fosdick have been replaced by Tracy's extremely complex account of the hermeneutics of a classic expression of religious experience. Nor to find Kaufman saying in his most recent book: "I am not addressing the question whether some being named 'God' actually exists, but rather am setting out certain aspects of the meaning or content which, in our religious and cultural traditions, the symbol 'God' has come to bear."[40]

Conclusions like Barth's remain an important reason for the rejection of experiential foundationalism by conservatives. It is telling that in McGrath's textbook he ends the discussion of religious experience as a source of theology with a discussion of Feuerbach.[41] In *The Genesis of Doctrine* he says that there is a question that demands attention:

---

36. Friedrich Schleiermacher, *The Christian Faith*, ed. H. R. Mackintosh and J. S. Steward (Edinburgh: T. & T. Clark, 1960), 67. First published 1821-22.

37. Ludwig Feuerbach, in *Das Wesen des Religion*, trans. by George Eliot as *The Essence of Christianity*.

38. Welch, *Protestant Thought in the Nineteenth Century*, 2:173.

39. See Karl Barth, *Church Dogmatics* (Edinburgh: T. & T. Clark, 1936-1969), I/ 2:288-91.

40. Kaufman, *In Face of Mystery*, 8.

41. McGrath, *Christian Theology*, 199-200.

How can we know that—how, in fact, can we even begin to inquire whether, and in what manner—the experience we are attempting to capture in a verbal moment or symbol really is an experience *of God.* What grounds do we have for suggesting that human experience is in some way related to a reality, traditionally designated 'God'? On what grounds are we entitled to identify a moment or moments as charged with the fragrance of divinity, and not simply an experience which is human and mundane? (24).

OUTSIDE-IN THEOLOGIES

Thomas Reid was the founder of a philosophical school called common-sense realism. Reid, a critic of Hume, recognized that Hume's skepticism was essentially a result of his inside-out epistemology. Hume had pointed out that if we begin with our sensory impressions, considered as mental contents, there is no justifiable way to argue—by induction or causal reasoning—to conclusions about the external world. Reid thus rejected the "idea idea," the view that all we are ever aware of is our own mental representations of reality. In doing so, Reid claimed to be speaking for ordinary people, who do not suppose that their sensations must *resemble* objects if they are to have knowledge of those objects. They do not suppose that the sensations in their fingers when grasping an apple are anything like roundness. Similarly, what we mean by *red* is not the sensation in our minds when we look at an apple but is rather the property in the apple that produces this sensation.

So sensations are accounted for in an outside-in manner in terms of the properties of objects rather than the reverse. Furthermore, Reid rejects the inside-out view that one must *argue* from sensations to truths about objects. We have simply been constituted by God in such a way that we pass immediately from sensations to beliefs about the objects that cause them.

This move itself might have accounted for Reid's position being called common sense, but the label actually comes from his view that God has implanted in all human beings certain beliefs, such as the existence of the external world and other minds, the uniformity of nature, and the existence of God. These are principles of "common sense," which need no proof because anyone who really doubted them would be mad.

Reid's influence on conservative theology is seen very directly in arguments such as Charles Hodge's that knowledge of God's existence is innate. But Reid's greatest effect was to shore up the Princeton school's confidence in our in-built ability to perceive facts—facts of all sorts—and to know reality directly. Beginning with Augustine's metaphor of the two books, nature and the Bible, Charles Hodge argued for a theological epistemology exactly parallel to Reid's scientific epistemology. Just as Reid predicated confidence in the testimony of the senses on the trustworthiness of God, so Hodge predicated confidence in the testimony of the Scriptures on their status as the word of God.

Archibald Hodge and B. B. Warfield later replied to the introduction of historical-critical study of the Bible by asserting that just as the truth about nature was accessible by means of an ordinary looking and seeing, similarly the facts of the Bible were accessible to a disciplined but ordinary process of reading and understanding.[42]

The two-books metaphor also led Princeton theologians to apply to theology current theories of scientific reasoning. They made great use of the inductivist view of scientific method, whose most significant early proponent was Francis Bacon (1561-1626), and which was further promulgated by John Stuart Mill (1806-73). According to the inductivists, scientific reasoning involves the formation of general principles (including causal hypotheses) on the basis of observable facts. The following quotations from Charles Hodge reflect, first, his acceptance of Reid's principles of common sense and, second, his adoption of an inductive theory of scientific and theological reasoning:

> *The Inductive Method* . . . is so called because it agrees in everything essential with the inductive method as applied to the natural sciences.
>
> First, The man of science comes to the study of nature with certain assumptions. (1.) He assumes the trustworthiness of his sense perceptions. . . . The facts of nature reveal themselves to our faculties of sense, and can be known in no other way. (2.) He must also assume the trustworthiness of his mental operations. He must take for granted that he can perceive, compare, combine, remember, and infer; and that he can safely rely upon these mental faculties in their legitimate exercise. (3.) He must also rely on the certainty of those truths which are not learned from experience, but which are given in the constitu-

---

42. These parallels are drawn by James B. Miller and Dean R. Fowler in "What's Wrong with the Creation/Evolution Controversy?," *Center for Theology and the Natural Sciences Bulletin* 4 (Autumn 1984): 1-13. See, for example, Charles Hodge's comments on the perspicuity of Scripture in *Systematic Theology*, 1:183-85. However, this is not to say that the Princeton theologians rejected all critical methods; see Warfield's *Textual Criticism of the New Testament* (New York: Thomas Whittaker, 1887). Even here the scientific language and the emphasis on the plain sense appear; regarding disagreements in labeling textual errors: "We must neither allow ourselves so to sharpen our acuteness that we discern an error in every corner, and lose the power to catch the plain intent of a plain man's plain speech. . . . The whole matter is nevertheless simply a matter of fact, and is to be determined solely by the evidence, investigated under the guidance of reverential and candid good sense" (208).

tion of our nature. That every effect must have a cause; that the same cause under like circumstances, will produce like effects. . . .

Second, The student of nature having this ground on which to stand, and these tools wherewith to work, proceeds to perceive, gather, and combine his facts. These he does not pretend to manufacture, nor presume to modify. . . . He is only careful to be sure that they are real, and that he has them all, or, at least all that are necessary to justify any inference which he may draw from them, or any theory which he may build upon them.

Third, From facts thus ascertained and classified, he deduces the laws by which they are determined. . . .

The Bible is to the theologian what nature is to the man of science. It is his store-house of facts; and his method of ascertaining what the Bible teaches, is the same as that which the natural philosopher adopts to ascertain what nature teaches. In the first place he comes to his task with all the assumptions above mentioned. . . .

In the second place, the duty of the Christian theologian is to ascertain, collect, and combine all the facts which God has revealed concerning himself and our relation to Him. These facts are all in the Bible. . . .

In the third place, the theologian must be guided by the same rules in the collection of facts, as govern the man of science. . . .

In the fourth place, in theology as in natural science, principles are derived from facts, and not impressed upon them. . . .

It is the fundamental principle of all sciences, and of theology among the rest, that theory is to be determined by facts, and not facts by theory. As natural science was a chaos until the principle of induction was admitted and faithfully carried out, so theology is a jumble of human speculations, not worth a straw, when men refuse to apply the same principle to the study of the Word of God.[43]

A. H. Strong's advocacy of an outside-in approach in contrast to inside-out is seen in the following:

Even if religious ideas sprang wholly from within, an external revelation might stir up the dormant powers of the mind. Religious ideas, however, do not spring wholly from within. External revelation can impart them. Man can reveal himself to man by external communications, and, if God has equal power with man, God can reveal himself to man in like manner.[44]

---

43. Charles Hodge, *Systematic Theology*, 1:9-15.
44. Strong, *Systematic Theology*, 12.

So, in contrast to the liberal, inside-out approach to theological method, the conservatives have established an outside-in methodology. Theology begins with the facts of the Bible; the Christian's (inner) knowledge of God is based on that external authority. But the problem that exercised Locke is still with us some two hundred years later: how to know (with the requisite foundational certainty) that the Bible is indeed the indubitable revelation of God.

SUMMARY

I have argued that two philosophical theories about the nature of knowledge have shaped modern conceptions of theological method. Each theory has provided (Protestant) theologians with only two live options. First, foundationalism sent theologians in search of an indubitable starting point for theology, and there turned out to be only two possibilities, Scripture or a special sort of religious experience.

Second, if theories of knowledge can be classified as either inside-out or outside-in, this again gives theologians only two options. But these options cannot be mixed and matched at will. On the one hand, the conservatives' choice of Scripture for their foundation—an *external* authority—meant that they needed something like Reid's outside-in approach to knowledge. On the other hand, the kind of experience demanded by experiential foundationalism is an *inner* experience, and thus the liberals found themselves with an inside-out approach to theology. So the options for theologians in the modern period seem to have come down to two.

2

Description or Expression

How Can We Speak about God?

INTRODUCTION

In 1955 the philosopher R. B. Braithwaite proposed what many would take
to be an outlandish theory of religious language. When Christians assert, for
example, that "God is love," they are not in fact speaking about God but
rather about themselves. Religious language (as does moral language, according to Braithwaite) *expresses* the speaker's *intentions.* Here the intention is to live in a loving manner, to lead an "agapeistic" life. In addition,
Christians tell stories about Jesus and his followers, which need not be true
accounts, since their real function is to serve as psychological reinforcement
for the intention to live in a Christian manner.[1]

This chapter examines two very different theories of the nature of religious language: the propositional and the experiential-expressivist theories.[2]
In the accounts so far presented of the liberal and conservative types of
theology, it is already apparent that they include different understandings of
language. Conservatives emphasize the *factual* nature of religious language.
Those who hold inerrantist doctrines of Scripture emphasize *verbal* inspiration, suggesting not only that the content is *literally* true, but that the very
words were revealed by God. In contrast, the liberal type of theologian speaks
in terms of the *aptness* or *adequacy* of religious language to describe reli-

---

1. R. B. Braithwaite, *An Empiricist's View of the Nature of Religious Belief* (Cambridge: Cambridge University Press, 1955); for an account of Braithwaite's views
see James Wm. McClendon, Jr., and James M. Smith, *Understanding Religious
Convictions* (Notre Dame: University of Notre Dame Press, 1974), 23-29.

2. George Lindbeck coined the term *experiential-expressivist* to describe a theory
of the nature of religion and doctrine. See *The Nature of Doctrine: Religion and
Theology in a Postliberal Age* (Philadelphia: Westminster Press, 1984).

gious experience—to *express* religious awareness—and takes this adequacy to be a matter of degree.

There is a striking correlation between these two approaches to language among theologians and a comparable pair of theories of language developed by philosophers in the late modern period. We shall call these the referential and expressivist theories. It would be anachronistic to claim that these two twentieth-century philosophical theories influenced the development of liberal and conservative forms of theology, since the two theological traditions were well developed before their philosophical counterparts. However, recall the suggestion (in the Introduction) that philosophy often serves to uncover assumptions already implicit in a worldview. If this is the case, then we can say that early modern *assumptions* about language—that it must be either representative or expressive—later became explicit in two areas: in philosophers' theories and in the development of two different conceptions of theology. We saw in the preceding chapter that modern theories of knowledge created a forced option for theologians. Modern assumptions about language set up another pair of options. After we have examined the limited possibilities, we shall see why a theory such as Braithwaite's might have seemed appealing.

There are intimate connections between theories of language and theories of knowledge. The thesis of this chapter, then, is that contrasting assumptions about religious language (describable in terms of two modern philosophical theories) contribute to the gulf between liberal and conservative theological positions. These differences are closely tied to the epistemological options described in Chapter 1. The two options can be represented as in Table 1 below:

	Liberal	*Conservative*
knowledge	experiential foundationalism inside-out	scriptural foundationalism outside-in
language	expressivism	propositionalism

Table 1.

Finally, in this chapter we shall consider how the two opposing theories of religious language result in strikingly different positions on two controversial issues: The first is the use of gender-linked language in speaking about God. The second concerns the relationship between Christianity and science. Conservatives are noted for their perception of conflict between theology and science, especially evolutionary biology. This conflict is made possible by their propositional view of religious language. Liberal theology has been largely shaped by accommodation to modern science, beginning with Newton's physics. To a great extent this accommodation has been made possible by the experiential-expressivist theory of language.

MODERN PHILOSOPHY OF LANGUAGE

By the early decades of the twentieth century, philosophy of language had become a central focus of Anglo-American philosophy. Richard Rorty speaks of "the linguistic turn," the judgment that philosophical problems could best be addressed by attending to language.[3] This supplanted the turn to epistemology, which marked the beginning of the modern period. To illustrate, we might say that whereas ancient and medieval philosophers asked metaphysical questions about what there is, early modern philosophers recognized a prior question: how can we *know* what exists? Late modern philosophers ask: what do we *mean* when we say that we know something? (or, what are the *linguistic categories* needed to give a complete account of what there is?).

It should not be surprising, then, that a great deal of attention has been given in the twentieth century to the development of explicit theories about language, answering especially the question: how does language get its meaning? Or, better: what is the meaning of *meaning*? The predominant modern answer has been what could be called either the referential or the representative theory: words get their meaning from the things in the world to which they *refer*, or sentences get their meaning from the facts or states of affairs they *represent*.

However, with this clear referential approach to language came the recognition that whole realms of discourse, such as ethics and aesthetics, were not, in this sense, meaningful. This prompted the elaboration of a second theory of language—or, more precisely, the elaboration of a theory of *second-class* language. Here the emphasis is on the function of language to express the emotions, attitudes, or intentions of the speaker. Hence, this theory could be called expressivist or emotivist. We look at the referential and expressivist theories in turn.

Ludwig Wittgenstein begins his *Philosophical Investigations* with a quotation from Augustine's *Confessions* in which Augustine describes how he imagines he learned language.

> When they (my elders) named some object, and accordingly moved towards something, I saw this and I grasped that the thing was called by the sound they uttered when they meant to point it out. . . . Thus, as I heard words repeatedly used in their proper places in various sentences, I gradually learnt to understand what objects they signified; and after I had trained my mouth to form these signs, I used them to express my own desires. (*Confessions*, I, 8.)

Wittgenstein comments:

---

3. Richard Rorty, ed., *The Linguistic Turn* (Chicago: University of Chicago Press, 1967).

These words, it seems to me, give us a particular picture of the essence of human language. It is this: the individual words in language name objects—sentences are combinations of such names. —In this picture of language we find the roots of the following idea: Every word has a meaning. This meaning is correlated with the world. It is the object for which the word stands.[4]

So here Wittgenstein is acknowledging a common-sense view that to know the meaning of a word is to know the object to which it refers—a view that goes back at least to Augustine.

Philosophical attempts to understand language have typically been somewhat more complicated than this common-sense view. For John Locke, at the beginning of the modern period, words referred to or represented ideas: "Words in their primary or immediate signification, stand for nothing but the ideas in the mind of him that uses them."[5] Ideas, in turn, stood for things; simple ideas were "perfectly taken from the existence of things."[6] Simple ideas were compounded to form complex ideas; sentences represented the connections the mind makes between ideas.

The German philosopher and mathematician Gottlob Frege (1848-1925) has probably done more than anyone to shape late-modern theories of language. First, he rejected "psychologism," the view that the meaning of language has anything to do with any sort of mental process (for example, Locke's "ideas"). Since Frege, philosophers have concentrated on the two-term relation between language and the world rather than the three-term relation among language, the mind, and the world.

Second, Frege argued that a theory of meaning cannot begin with individual terms. He claimed that it is only within the context of a sentence that words have determinate meanings. The meaning of a word consists in the contribution it makes to the meaning of an entire sentence. This solves the problem of the reference of words such as *not* and *sake*.

Another early-twentieth-century contribution to referential theories of meaning was the logical positivists' verification theory, according to which the meaning of a sentence is given in the observations that would verify or falsify it. Logical positivism is a philosophical movement that grew out of the work of the Vienna Circle: mathematicians, logicians, scientists, and others, meeting between 1922 and 1936. An allied movement called logical atomism developed in Britain around the same time. Both of these movements were strongly empiricist, in the tradition of Hume, and anti-metaphysical. Both took the analysis of language to be the primary method of philosophy. The verification criterion was meant to explain how empirical

---

4. Ludwig Wittgenstein, *Philosophical Investigations*, trans. G. E. M. Anscombe (New York: Macmillan, 1953), §1.

5. John Locke, *An Essay Concerning Human Understanding* (1690), III, ii, 2.

6. Ibid., iv, 17.

language gets its meaning but also to identify metaphysical discourse and rule it out as meaningless.

A. J. Ayer (1910-1989) did more than anyone else to promote the views of the logical atomists and the Vienna Circle in the English-speaking world. His *Language, Truth and Logic*[7] has been judged one of the most influential books of the century.[8] Ayer classes sentences into three types: those that are empirically meaningful; those that are true by definition (tautologies); and the rest, merely expressive of emotion.

> The criterion which we use to test the genuineness of apparent state-ments of fact is the criterion of verifiability. We say that a sentence is factually significant to any given person, if, and only if, he knows how to verify the proposition which it purports to express—that is, if he knows what observations would lead him, under certain conditions, to accept the proposition as being true, or reject it as being false. If, on the other hand, the putative proposition is of such a character that the assumption of its truth, or falsehood, is consistent with any assump-tion whatsoever concerning the nature of his future experience, then, as far as he is concerned, it is, if not a tautology, a mere pseudo-propo-sition. The sentence expressing it may be emotionally significant to him; but it is not literally significant (35).

So here the distinction appears between two kinds of language: that which is meaningful because it describes some (actual or possible) observable state of affairs, and that which has merely emotional significance. The impor-tance for Ayer of recognizing emotive language is that it allows him to ad-dress the criticism that his theory of language cannot account for value judg-ments, either ethical or aesthetic. Ayer's theory of ethical language is illustrated by the following example:

> If I were to say to someone, "You acted wrongly in stealing that money," I am not stating anything more than if I had simply said, "You stole that money." In adding that this action is wrong I am not making any further statement about it. I am simply evincing my moral disapproval of it. It is as if I had said, "You stole that money," in a peculiar tone of horror, or written it with the addition of some special exclamation marks. The tone, or the exclamation marks, adds nothing to the literal meaning of the sentence. It merely serves to show that the expression of it is attended by certain feelings in the speaker (107).

---

7. Alfred Jules Ayer, *Language, Truth and Logic* (1936); quotations below are from the second edition (New York: Dover Publications, 1952).

8. By D. J. O'Connor, in *Encyclopedia of Philosophy* (1967), s.v. "Alfred Jules Ayer."

In addition to their function of expressing emotions, moral words serve to arouse such feelings and so to stimulate actions.

Ayer goes on to discuss religious language and to argue that it is utterly devoid of meaning, but one can see how easy it would be to take Ayer's account of emotive language and apply it to religion. The only question is, if moral language expresses feelings of approval, disapproval, admiration, horror, what sorts of inward realities does religious language express? Braithwaite's answer was to assimilate religious to moral language and to claim that both express *intentions* regarding policies of action. Among theological accounts we shall find a vast array of proposals.

THREE MODELS OF RELIGION

George Lindbeck made a significant contribution to the discussion of theological theories of religious language in *The Nature of Doctrine*. The book grew out of Lindbeck's participation in ecumenical dialogue and an attempt to determine what representatives of various Christian communions could mean in saying both that they had come to agreement on points of doctrine which used to divide and that their churches had not changed their traditional teachings. So Lindbeck's book is a study of different theories about doctrine and the nature of religions. He describes three such theories:

> One of these emphasizes the cognitive aspects of religion and stresses the ways in which church doctrines function as informative propositions or truth claims about objective realities. Religions are thus thought of as similar to philosophy or science as these were classically conceived. This was the approach of traditional orthodoxies (as well as of many heterodoxies), but it also has certain affinities to the outlook on religion adopted by much modern Anglo-American analytic philosophy with its preoccupation with the cognitive or informational meaningfulness of religious utterances (16).

Lindbeck associates the second type of theory with the liberal tradition:

> A second approach focuses on what I shall call in this book the "experiential-expressive" dimension of religion, and it interprets doctrines as noninformative and nondiscursive symbols of inner feelings, attitudes, or existential orientations. This approach highlights the resemblances of religions to aesthetic enterprises and is particularly congenial to the liberal theologies influenced by the Continental developments that began with Schleiermacher (16).

Lindbeck develops a third account of religion and doctrine. According to this "cultural-linguistic" theory, religions resemble languages or cultures.

Doctrines are "regulative"; they are communally authoritative rules that govern attitude, action, and the use of first-order religious language.

Each of these three understandings of doctrine and religion—the "cognitive-propositional," the "experiential-expressive," and the "cultural-linguistic"—incorporates a view of the nature of religious language. We shall only be concerned with the propositional and experiential-expressivist theories of language in this chapter; we consider Lindbeck's own views in Chapter 5. My indebtedness to Lindbeck for this terminology is obvious.

One point at which my account differs from Lindbeck's is with regard to the question of how the three theories of religion are related historically. Lindbeck calls his cultural-linguistic model postmodern and postliberal; in addition, he gives very little attention to the cognitive model, seeming to suppose that all but the analytic philosophers have abandoned it in favor of the more recent experiential-expressivist model. Thus, the cognitive model is premodern, the experiential-expressivist model is modern, and the cultural-linguistic model is postmodern.[9]

However, my goal in the first three chapters of this book is to show that there are two models of religion, and two theological traditions, that are equally modern in their presuppositions. In particular, the goal of the following sections is to show that the liberals' experiential-expressivist theories of religious language are instances of the more general expressivist theory of language, and that the propositional theory is an instance of the predominant modern referential theory of language.[10]

PROPOSITIONAL THEORIES OF LANGUAGE IN CONSERVATIVE THEOLOGY

The propositional theory of religious language correlates directly with modern referential theories of language. The only difference is that whereas Ayer and company insisted that meaningful language must refer to and describe realities available to the five senses (and thus promoted a materialistic metaphysic), conservative theologians recognize immaterial realities as well and claim that these are the primary referents of religious language. Doctrines, if true, refer to and accurately represent these supra-empirical states of affairs. Charles Hodge emphasizes the parallels between scientific facts and scriptural facts: "The duty of the Christian theologian is to ascertain, collect, and combine all the facts which God has revealed concerning him-

---

9. An exception is contemporary Catholic theology, such as that of Karl Rahner and Bernard Lonergan, who, Lindbeck says, attempt to combine the experiential-expressivist and propositionalist accounts.

10. I do not venture to give an account of premodern conceptions, but I suspect that the modern propositionalist view has closer relations to ancient and medieval views of religious language than does the experiential-expressivist.

self and our relation to Him."[11] So propositional theories of religious la...
guage assume that the primary function of religious language is to describe
God and God's relation to the world and to humankind; for example, the
doctrine of creation is stating a fact about how the universe came into being, namely, that it was by an act of God.

The most extreme form of propositionalism is found in the writings of
A. A. Hodge, who claims that even the choice of words in Scripture is governed by divine inspiration:

> [By verbal inspiration] is meant that the divine influence, of whatever
> kind it may have been, which accompanied the sacred writers in what
> they wrote, extends to their expression of their thoughts in language,
> as well as to the thoughts themselves. The effect being that in the origi-
> nal autograph copies the language expresses the thought God intended
> to convey with infallible accuracy, so that the words as well as the
> thoughts are God's revelation to us.[12]

A. H. Strong's view of religious language is equally referential. He speaks
of theology as aiming to ascertain the facts respecting God and God's relation to the universe, and to exhibit these facts in their rational unity (2).
However, he is somewhat more guarded about the adequacy of human language to represent spiritual truths (35), rejecting A. A. Hodge's view that
God provides the language directly by means of revelation:

> Inspiration did not always, or even generally, involve a direct commu-
> nication to the Scripture writers of the words they wrote. . . . The Scrip-
> ture writers appear to have been so influenced by the Holy Spirit that
> they perceived and felt even the new truths they were to publish, as
> discoveries of their own minds, and were left to the action of their own
> minds in the expression of these truths, with the single exception that
> they were supernaturally held back from the selection of wrong words,
> and when needful were provided with right ones.[13]

Strong's understanding of language precedes the Fregean rejection of concepts as a middle term in the relation between words and their referents:
"Language is the expression of general notions by symbols. . . . Words are
the symbols of concepts. Where there are no concepts there can be no words"
(467).

---

11. Charles Hodge, *Systematic Theology*, 1:11.

12. A. A. Hodge, *Outlines of Theology*, enl. ed. (Grand Rapids, MI: Eerdmans,
1949), 66-67. First published 1878.

13. Strong, *Systematic Theology*, 216. The last sentence strikes this reader as an
ad hoc move to protect theology's *foundation* from challenge—unwarranted but
quite understandable.

When we reach the contemporary period, we find conservative theologians continuing to insist on the cognitive, referential nature of religious language but acknowledging even more than did Strong the inadequacy of human language for religious purposes. Alister McGrath states that "the transcendent can never be wholly captured in finite language, so that we are obliged to rely upon images and models which elude precise definition."[14]

One chapter of McGrath's *Genesis of Doctrine* contains a response to Lindbeck's account of the cognitive-propositionalist type. McGrath's first criticism is that Lindbeck has failed to note the awareness of theologians of this type of the relative inadequacy of religious language—the very point just noted regarding McGrath himself, and a feature that we have already seen beginning to appear in Strong's theology. "It is necessary," says McGrath, "to make a clear distinction between the view that an exhaustive and unambiguous account of God is transmitted conceptually by propositions on the one hand, and the view that there is a genuinely cognitive dimension, component, or element to doctrinal statements on the other" (20). McGrath rejects the former position but insists on the latter.

To clarify his stand on the representational character of religious language, McGrath compares his views to positions regarding scientific language:

> There are important and illuminating connections here with recent debates within the philosophy of the natural sciences concerning the status of theoretical terms. An instrumentalist interpretation of theoretical terms argues that theories relate to phenomena, to human perceptions, to *observabilia,* without making reference to what is 'really out there.' A realist interpretation, however, carries with it a commitment to a belief in the reality of those things which constitute the denotation of the terms of the theoretical language of that theory (31).

McGrath criticizes Lindbeck's cultural-linguistic position as a form of instrumentalism. He compares his own to that of the realist, but we should say, more precisely, that his position corresponds to that of critical realists in philosophy of science, who wish to maintain a referential, representative view of language, but recognize, as does McGrath, that our language is not entirely adequate for that task.[15]

McGrath recognizes that there is more to religious language than the cognitive element; there is an existential (self-involving) element as well. However, he argues that it is a mistake so to emphasize the existential as to deny the cognitive:

---

14. McGrath, *The Genesis of Doctrine*, 3.

15. I speak of critical realists as "chastened moderns." See Nancey Murphy, "Scientific Realism and Postmodern Philosophy," *British Journal for Philosophy of Science* 41 (1990): 291-303.

There is an ineradicable cognitive element in Christian doctrine. . . . It purports to be a representation, however inadequate or provisional. . . . In declaring that "God is love," for example, I am not merely declaring my allegiance to a community that affirms that "God is love," irrespective of what God may actually be like. Nor am I merely affirming a broad positive personal attitude to God, irrespective of what he may actually be like. I am affirming that I understand that "God is love" [is] an authentic and valid insight into the character of God, and that this belief is grounded, and the hitherto undefined concept of "love" implicated therein is instantiated, in the history of Jesus of Nazareth" (75-76).

So that to which religious language refers is primarily God and God's dealings with humanity, especially in Jesus. The primary religious language of the Scriptures is thus narrative in form, recounting God's actions. Myth and metaphor are often used in Scripture, but these are non-literal forms of *representation*. Doctrinal language is conceptual language, appropriate to its historical context, which provides an interpretation of the realities described in the scriptural narrative.

Donald Bloesch's account of scriptural language is interesting in that he is struggling to incorporate insights of the expressivist view and yet maintain an uncompromised propositionalism.

Although open to the insights of existentialists and neo-orthodox theologies, I have sought to retain the conceptual character of revelation even while subordinating it to personal self-disclosure. As I see it, revelation is God's self-communication through his selected instrumentality, especially the inspired witness of his prophets and apostles. This act of self-communication entails not only the unveiling of his gracious and at the same time awesome presence but also the imparting of the knowledge of his will and purpose for humankind. This knowledge is conceptual as well as existential and can be formulated but never possessed in propositions.
    . . . Revelation is indeed cognitive, but it is much more than this.
    . . . It . . . involves not only the mind but also the will and affections.[16]

Bloesch's struggle comes across most clearly in his discussion of mythological language. He recognizes that much of the biblical language has a mythological character. However, he rejects the view that myth speaks of universal human experience rather than of history. In response to Rudolf Bultmann, he maintains that

the New Testament myth is theological and not anthropological. Its principal purpose is not to lead us to self-understanding but to de-

---

16. Bloesch, *Holy Scripture*, 48.

scribe the mighty acts of God recorded in history. Bultmann overlooked the fact that mythopoetic language is the only possible medium for speaking about God's activity. To translate myth into a philosophical conceptuality is to risk losing sight of the reality the myth describes and proclaims (237).

Myth is a figurative representation of a reality that eludes precise description or definition. The biblical writers began with historical facts but added mythological allusions, thus giving the facts more than simply historical significance (262). The "more" here is the figurative description of the dramatic interaction between divinity and humanity, an interaction that cannot be captured in literal, univocal language (266).

In the next chapter we take up the issue of divine action. One statement by Bloesch will serve to preview conclusions there about the connections between theories of religious language and theories of divine action:

> We must take care to differentiate this understanding of myth from that held by Bultmann, Willi Marxsen, Ernst Käsemann and other rationalistic critics. In contrast to Bultmann I contend that the mythopoetic imagery of the Bible is not the projection of inner experiences on the plane of history but a vehicle *by which the objective intrusion of God into history is described* [italics added] (266).

EXPRESSIVIST THEORIES OF LANGUAGE IN LIBERAL THEOLOGY

When Friedrich Schleiermacher wrote in *The Christian Faith* that religion is neither a knowing nor a doing, but a matter of feeling; that religious affections are a form of self-consciousness; and that "Christian doctrines are accounts of the Christian religious affections set forth in speech,"[17] he inaugurated a true revolution in theology. There is no aspect of the liberal tradition that reflects more clearly the radicality of this move than its understanding of religious language. As mentioned above, Lindbeck has coined the term *experiential-expressive* to refer to this conception of the nature of religion and of doctrine, but the term applies equally well to the liberal type's theory of religious language. There is some basic *experience* (described differently by different theologians) that constitutes the essence of religion; religious language gives *expression* to this experience. However, there may also be second-order religious language of a more conceptual nature, which evaluates and orders primary religious language. So, for example, according to Schleiermacher, the doctrine of creation does not describe God's acts in creating the universe but expresses the Christian's awareness of the depend-

---

17. Schleiermacher, *The Christian Faith*, §§3, 5, 15.

ence of all things upon God. Second-order theological language involves claims such as that the doctrine of creation, so understood, is a legitimate expression of the Christian's religious awareness.

Harry Emerson Fosdick speaks of "the fundamental experiences of men's spirit."[18] Here he has in mind fairly common sorts of religious experience: sin and its consequences, hunger for righteousness, love, hate and jealousy, heartbreak, grief and tragedy, joy, hope, and the need for God (56). Fosdick, the preacher, is noted for catchy turns of phrase, and one that has endured is his claim that in Scripture we find "abiding experiences set in changing categories" (96). Thus, the job of the preacher is to decode the abiding meanings of Scripture, strip them of their outgrown phraseology, and translate them into modern categories. This theme of *translation* is a common one in modern theology.

Shailer Mathews presents a similar but more detailed expressivist account of language in *The Faith of Modernism*. Religion is essentially a matter of spiritual experience, attitudes (such as faith or trust), and one's private moral convictions. The Bible is a record of the historical development of such experiences and attitudes. (Note the contrast with the conservative account of the Bible as a record of divine action.) The literary forms in the Bible reflect their own times. It does not matter if biblical stories turn out to be legendary; "this would simply mean that the past expressed its religious attitude and conviction by the use of legend" (45). Historical study of the Bible aims at recapturing the experience of the biblical writers. Doctrinal language is expressive also:

> If we are to understand our religion we must, therefore, do more than study its formulas and institutions. We must look beneath and through the Creeds and Confessions to the attitudes and convictions, the needs, temptations and trials, the prayer and rites, in a word, the actual religious life of the ongoing and developing Christian group. We must discover when a doctrine arose, for what purpose it was organized, what religious attitude it expressed, what unifying social practice or idea it used as a "pattern." From such a study the conclusion will be clear that while formulas are a part of our religion they are not to be identified with that religion. They spring from the effort of Christians in different situations to organize their lives and carry their daily burdens, perform their varying tasks, not only with prayer and sacrifice but in loyalty to the inherited attitudes and convictions of their group regarding God and Jesus Christ.
>
> . . . A study of the origin and purpose of our doctrines shows how patterns have originated and served actual needs of a group. By them attitudes and convictions are given expression in doctrines (58-59).

---

18. Fosdick, *The Modern Use of the Bible*, 54.

Note the pragmatist tendencies here—the account of doctrines in terms of their social and religious *functions*. This pragmatism comes out more directly in Mathews's account of how doctrinal formulations are tested for adequacy. In the past, doctrines achieved the status of orthodoxy because they satisfied the religious needs of an evolving social order (65). "A doctrine, historically considered, is true when in an effective pattern it expresses and legitimates the Christian group's faith in Jesus as Savior" (73). The utility of doctrines is not merely to express faith in ways suited to the current social order, but also to inspire experiences, attitudes, and social action (83).

Here we come very close to an account of religious language parallel to Ayer's account of moral language. Religious language expresses attitudes and personal moral convictions, and at the same time aims to arouse feelings and so to stimulate action.

Contemporary expressivist accounts of language are more complex. Recall that for David Tracy the task of theology is to correlate the "meanings" present in common human experience and language with the "meanings" present in the Christian tradition.[19] The word *meanings* seems to do double duty here, referring both to experiences of the meaningfulness or significance of various aspects of life and to verbal expressions of that experience.[20]

Investigation of the Christian tradition pertains primarily to the existential meanings expressed in the New Testament's christological texts, in which metaphors, symbols, and images are used to express the religious significance of the proclamation that Jesus is the Christ. Tracy speaks of the "referents" of the text, and this is a term one would expect a propositionalist to use. However, these referents do not consist in "the meanings 'behind' the text," for example, "the author's *real* intention or the socio-cultural situation of the text." Rather, the referent is "the meaning 'in front of' the text, i.e., that way of perceiving reality, that mode of being-in-the-world which the text opens up" (51). The basic mode of being-in-the-world that the Christian texts open up Tracy describes as living "as though in the presence of a gracious God" (52).

So here Tracy is using the term *referent* in a way diametrically opposed to that of the propositional or referential theory of the conservatives: he uses it to develop a thoroughly expressivist account of scriptural language. Scriptural language, if meaningful, expresses a way of experiencing reality that can be called religious.

However, Tracy does raise a question of reference in the usual sense. If religious faith consists in living *as if* in the presence of a gracious God, does this require that there *be* such a God? After recognizing that for some (Buddhists, and even some Christians) it does not, he affirms that the theistic question "is capable of receiving a positive answer" (54). But this is not

---

19. As developed in *Blessed Rage for Order*.

20. I offer this interpretation tentatively, however, since I am not at all sure I have adequately grasped Tracy's meaning.

possible prior to an examination of the religious dimension of common human experience.

In everyday life, in science, when reflecting on our moral lives, we become aware of limits or boundaries. Encounters with death or sickness cause us to experience our basic finitude and contingency. Limit experiences raise limit questions; for example, can the world be intelligible to science if it has no intelligent ground? Is it worthwhile to ask whether our goals, purposes, and ideals are themselves worthwhile? (98) These experiences and questions disclose our basic faith (or unfaith) in the worthwhileness of existence. To have such faith is to have the religious attitude.

> Religious language does not present a new, supernatural world wherein we may escape the only world we know or wish to know. Rather that language re-presents our always threatened basic confidence and trust in the very meaningfulness of even our most cherished and most noble enterprises, science, morality, and culture (135).

So the theologian's task is to interpret this basic faith in adequate categories but also to interpret in more adequate categories the faith expressed in the New Testament and to attempt to show that these two faiths are basically the same.

Tracy's account of religious language is heavily expressivist; one might say in the briefest possible terms that *what* religious language expresses is existential orientation. Yet religious language does make a limited cognitive claim:

> The principal cognitive claim involved in religious language . . . is the explicitly theistic claim: that the objective referent of all such language and experience is that reality which religious human beings mean when they say "God" (109).

Gordon Kaufman offers another version of expressivism. According to Kaufman the culture already possesses religious language; the theologian's job is to interpret and criticize it. So the question is, what is the nature and origin of this cultural religious language? In *An Essay on Theological Method* he says that theological terms are rooted in the wide *experience* of a whole culture; categories such as "God," "divine," "holy," have meaning only insofar as they succeed in both interpreting and forming experience. Theology, then,

> helps shape language into a vehicle which expresses our intentions with greater precision, thus facilitating a fuller and clearer consciousness of those intentions. . . . It searches out the rules governing the use of such talk so that it will be possible to see more clearly just what that talk is intending to express. Thus, theological analysis aims to distinguish better from worse forms of expression and seeks to define adequate or proper speech about God (9).

In his more recent work, *In Face of Mystery*, Kaufman has given more extensive consideration to the experience that religious language attempts to express and to the origin of religious language. As the title of the book suggests, he sees religion as a response to life's mystery: Who or what are we? With what realities have we to do in life? What meaning can human existence have?

> In the course of history many different views on these matters have appeared, and some of these have become formative of the great religious traditions. Within each tradition of commonly accepted symbols, rituals, and meanings, there is also much disagreement and argument. . . . Indeed, the symbol "God" . . . itself points to the great mystery of life, the deepest and most profound issues about which we do not know what to say. . . .
>
> Although the human spirit has no way of overcoming the mystery of life, it is also true that we are not able simply to live with a blank, empty Void. So humans create pictures, pictures of what they think the world is like, pictures of what they imagine are the ultimate powers or realities with which they must deal; and they create rituals through which they enact their own roles among these realities and powers. *We tell ourselves stories which depict the human situation in this world, and in our lives we attempt to act out our own parts in these stories.* Great imaginative pictures and stories and rituals of this sort have become collected in the historical traditions of value and meaning and practice which we know as the religions (29).[21]

While theology's task includes the interpretation of all religious symbols, its central focus in the West is the symbol "God." Kaufman emphasizes that this symbol derives only indirectly from experience. In *An Essay on Theological Method* he described the concept of God (in neo-Kantian fashion) as a regulative category whose function is to help organize all other categories. In *In Face of Mystery* he emphasizes that "God" names the point of reference in relation to which all else should be understood (9), a point from which to correct all human perspectives (8).

However, Kaufman writes:

> I am not addressing the question whether some being named "God" actually exists, but rather am setting out certain aspects of the meaning or content which, in our religious and cultural traditions, the symbol "God" has come to bear (8).

To make it clear that he is concerned with the symbol rather than whatever referent there may be, he alternates in the text, almost sentence by sentence,

---

21. Italics added; note the parallels with Braithwaite's theory of religious language.

between speaking of God and "God," where the latter designates the symbol.

So the two traditions, liberal and conservative, are in sharp disagreement over the nature of religious language—as much so now at the end of the modern period as at the beginning. On one side, there are those who affirm the "identity of the real and intended meanings of the biblical narratives, i.e., their literal meanings and their real meanings."[22] While some conservatives have softened their accounts of the factual accuracy and adequacy of religious language, they continue to maintain that the main purpose of religious language (biblical, doctrinal, and theological) is to refer to God and to describe God's actions, will, and intentions.

On the other side, the liberals began with the point that religious language cannot be *directly* about God but must be mediated—it must be, in the first instance, about how God appears in human subjectivity. The biblical narratives cannot be literally about God's doings; the real meaning must be about something else.[23] So theology comes to be described not as the science of God, but as the science of faith or of human religiosity, and this something else is the true referent of the biblical texts. But at the end of modernity, we find Tracy raising explicitly the question whether theistic language *has* a referent at all (apart from human experience). After a long and tortuous argument he answers that it does. But Kaufman is agnostic about the referent and is at pains to explain why that question need not be answered in order to do theology—it is not the existence of some being, but rather an adequate God-*concept* that is essential for human flourishing.[24]

CORRELATIONS WITH THEORIES OF KNOWLEDGE

Table 1 above represents the claim that experiential foundationalism and an inside-out approach to knowledge are strongly correlated with an expressivist theory of religious language, while scriptural foundationalism and an outside-in approach are correlated with a propositional view of language. We can easily see why this is the case. The propositionalists claim that religious language describes God and God's intentions. These are nonempirical (or "supra-empirical") realities. Even when we are describing God's acts in history, there is still a nonempirical element. For example, if we could see Jesus healing the paralytic with our own eyes, we would still not be able to see that it was done by the power of God. This is a point Bloesch makes in distinguishing between historical events and their revelational meaning.[25]

---

22. Hans Frei, *The Eclipse of Biblical Narrative: A Study in Eighteenth and Nineteenth Century Hermeneutics* (New Haven: Yale University Press, 1974), 64.

23. Ibid.

24. Kaufman, *In Face of Mystery*, 42.

25. Bloesch, *Holy Scripture*, 19.

So how can one *know* that the language accurately describes spiritual reality, or indeed, whether there is any such reality to describe? This question calls for a strong doctrine of revelation or inspiration; it must be an account of revelation as *God's* doing, not revelation in the sense in which we speak of a good idea coming "as a revelation," or of a work of art being "inspired." In other words, it must be an *outside-in* account of religious knowledge. So propositionalism *requires* an outside-in epistemology. And it coheres with scriptural-foundationalism because of the emphasis on revelation or inspiration.

Inside-out, experiential foundationalism *requires* an expressivist account of religious language. If the essence of religion is feeling, an *inner* awareness, then expressive language is really the only sort possible for first-order religious language. (Or at least it is the only interesting sort; one can imagine attempting to give a clinical report of the qualities of the experience itself, but this would have no religious value.) Religious experience does not come with precise descriptions attached. The human race must grope for adequate ways to communicate an awareness that is of a different order from awareness of the physical universe. The appropriate kind of language is symbolic, imagistic, metaphorical.

George Lindbeck criticizes experiential-expressivist theologians on the grounds that it is a mistake to believe that experience precedes language; rather, Lindbeck argues, language itself shapes experience. Lindbeck has been criticized, in turn, for attributing such a view of raw experience to Schleiermacher and his followers. Kaufman and Tracy both speak explicitly of the formative role of the language already available in religious traditions or the culture at large in inspiring and shaping religious experience. It seems clear that this recognition does go all the way back to Schleiermacher, for whom the Christian's awareness of absolute dependence is experienced in a manner already conditioned by the experience of Jesus Christ, transmitted through the community of the church.

So the experiential-expressivist claim that there is a *universal* human experience that serves as the ground of theology does not (necessarily or generally) involve the empirical claim that there is an experience phenomenologically the same in all cultures and traditions. Rather, it is a theoretical claim: there is an inward religiousness that manifests itself differently depending on cultural and linguistic conditioning, yet that which is so manifested is a universal human phenomenon.

However, when we put the experiential-expressivist position in this form, a question immediately arises: how can one *know* with the requisite foundational certainty that there is such a universal grounding beneath the varied manifestations or religious sensibilities that provide the immediate sources for theological reflection?[26] Thus, we find a besetting question parallel to

---

26. See Alister McGrath, *The Genesis of Doctrine*, 21-22.

that which plagues the conservatives: how can one know with the requisite certainty that the texts which provide the immediate source for theology are grounded by God's revelation?

THE BATTLE OVER INCLUSIVE LANGUAGE

A much disputed issue among theologians concerns the use of gender-linked language in speaking about God. Feminists object to the use of exclusively masculine language and images for God. Traditionalists object to any change in language. There is surely a variety of reasons and motives operative on both sides, but a large part of the dispute can be attributed to different theories about the nature of religious language; many (if not most) feminists fall within the liberal type with its expressivist theory of language, while traditionalists are often of the conservative type and hold a propositional view of religious language.

Feminists tend to emphasize the humanly contrived status of all religious language.[27] Feminist theologian Patricia Wilson-Kastner has provided a classic account of the expressivist theory:

> Theology and religious faith are not the same. Religious faith constitutes a fundamental personal relationship to the sacred. Faith may be expressed in a variety of physical, emotional, or intellectual ways, but they all spring from a primary, suprarational acceptance of the divine, rooted in a sense of the presence of the Ultimate to the self. Theology is the rational spelling-out and explaining of one's faith. There are many possible explanations, even for the same individual, and therefore many possible theologies. These theologies are influenced by point of view, questions raised by the individual and the culture of which the person is a part, the intellectual framework of the person formulating the theology, and so forth. Theology is a superstructure which arises from a faith, and expresses it on one significant but limited level. . . .
>
> If one were to search among other human acts for a comparison to the activity of faith, the best would be, I think, aesthetic experience. Insight, intuition, creativity, and appreciation—each has its analogue in a faith which both apprehends and feels itself grasped by the divine, reaches new depths of itself and others, and enjoys the beauty of all in light of the Ultimate. Theology, in this case, is most comparable to activities like aesthetics, or art or literary criticism. It is a limited, modest, always inadequate, but absolutely essential endeavor to explain intellectually what beauty is, how it is present in and to us, and how

---

27. Margo Houts, "Language, Gender, and God: How Traditionalists and Feminists Play the Inclusive Language Game," Ph.D. dissertation, Fuller Theological Seminary, 1993, 5.

we realize it. At the same time, to claim that any faith is perfect or any theology the final or full answer is as absurd as the notion that any artist has perfectly apprehended or expressed all beauty.[28]

Given a view of religious language such as this, it is perfectly reasonable to argue that masculine language and imagery are inappropriate for expressing women's faith experiences or that cultural changes involving the recognition and condemnation of patriarchy require reformulations of religious language. Rosemary Radford Ruether writes:

> The doctrine of Christ should be the most comprehensive way that Christians express their belief in redemption from all sin and evil in human life, the doctrine that embraces the authentic humanity and fulfilled hopes of all persons. . . . And yet, of all Christian doctrine, it has been the doctrine of Christ that has been most frequently used to exclude women from full participation in the Christian Church.[29]

The first such instance was the use of the term *logos* to define the presence of God in Jesus. She argues that this term has had an androcentric bias—rationality being associated with maleness in Greek culture.

After tracing later developments in Christology, Ruether turns to prescription:

> Thus we must say that the maleness of the historical Jesus has nothing to do with manifesting a male 'Son' who, in turn, images a male 'Father.' The divine 'Father' is equally mother. The 'Son' is equally daughter. Perhaps the parental language for transcendence and immanence itself should be relativized by some metaphor other than parent and child to better state this relationship between God transcendent and God manifest in creation and history (146-47).

We see repeated in Ruether's (and other feminists') work the concern of theologians of the liberal type (especially in pragmatic America) for the *effects* in the church and the social world of engineering linguistic changes. Ruether's practical concern is to dismantle oppressive hierarchies of gender, as well as of race, class, and culture.

In contrast, traditionalists emphasize the divinely revealed status of biblical language. The heirs of A. A. Hodge's tradition are wary about changing biblical patterns of speech, even when they reject Hodge's claim that the

---

28. Patricia Wilson-Kastner, *Faith, Feminism, and the Christ* (Philadelphia: Fortress Press, 1983), 6.

29. Rosemary Radford Ruether, "The Liberation of Christology from Patriarchy," in *Feminist Theology: A Reader*, ed. Ann Loades (Louisville, KY: Westminster/John Knox, 1990), 138.

very words are revealed by God. Donald Bloesch has devoted considerable effort to arguing against feminist proposals.[30] His propositional view entails that religious language conveys knowledge about the very nature of God. If one changes the language, one changes the concept of God and, in effect, establishes a new religion.

This claim is not at all surprising for one committed to the God-revealed, propositional character of biblical language. What is surprising is the lengths to which Bloesch is willing to go to avoid the theological implication of the feminine images for God in the Bible. Bloesch maintains that, while God is not male (a biological category), God is of masculine gender in the sense that "he chooses to relate to us in the form of the masculine—as Father, Son, and Holy Spirit."[31] So it is not appropriate to use feminine pronouns in reference to God or to call God "Mother."

So what about the feminine images? One move is to point out that masculine symbols predominate in the Bible. "He does not say so, but the inference is that if masculine symbols occur with greater frequency, they must be more appropriate or more valid."[32] In addition, Bloesch distinguishes between analogies and metaphors. He claims, first, that all of the masculine figures are analogies and the feminine figures metaphors; and second, that analogies tell us more about the referent than do metaphors. Analogies rest on actual similarities—for example, between God and human fathers—while metaphors merely suggest a similarity between two intrinsically unlike things.[33] So, clearly, while theories of language provide a partial explanation of differences between feminists and traditionalists, much more is going on here.

McGrath is one of the exceptions to the correlation of conservative theological type with traditionalism in gender language. He states that God is neither masculine nor feminine and reports with approval feminists' attempts to highlight the feminine images of God.[34]

RELATING RELIGION AND SCIENCE

A second difference between the liberal and conservative types of theology that can be understood by considering their different theories of language is

---

30. See Donald Bloesch, *Is the Bible Sexist? Beyond Feminism and Patriarchalism* (Westchester, IL: Crossway Books, 1982); idem, *The Battle for the Trinity: The Debate over Inclusive God-Language* (Ann Arbor, MI: Vine Books, 1985); and idem, *A Theology of Word and Spirit: Authority and Method in Theology* (Downers Grove, IL: InterVarsity Press, 1992).

31. Bloesch, *A Theology of Word and Spirit*, 91.

32. Houts, "Language, Gender, and God," 26.

33. Houts, *Language, Gender, and God,* 35; referring to Bloesch, *The Battle for the Trinity,* esp. page 21.

34. McGrath, *Christian Theology,* 205-7.

their different reactions to science. Conservatives are famous (or infamous) for their claims that modern science, especially evolutionary biology, is in conflict with Christian teaching. Liberals are equally well-known for having worked out means of accommodating theology to the modern world, beginning with attempts to come to terms with Newtonian physics. I do not mean to say that different theories of language *produced* different relations with science, only that we can see how these strikingly different relations are possible if we consider the theories of language. It would perhaps be more accurate to say that the liberals' concern to avoid conflict with science was a significant factor in producing the expressivist view of religious language.

As mentioned in the Introduction, much of the character of the liberal type of theology owes its inspiration to Immanuel Kant. Kant's philosophical project can be understood in terms of three goals: to protect Newtonian physics from David Hume's skepticism; to protect morality from the determinism of Newtonian physics; and to protect religion from both Humean skepticism and Newtonian determinism.

The problem of scientific determinism will be the focus of the next chapter, but some consideration is relevant here for understanding the liberal tradition's general response to science. Kant's strategy was to make a sharp distinction between the physical world as known to science and the moral world. Two different kinds of reasoning are involved: pure reason and practical reason, respectively. The (very limited) knowledge we can have of God is not a part of the sphere of pure reason. Thus, in Kant's view, there can be no natural theology, for example, knowledge of God derived from the order of the physical world. Rather, the existence of God is a postulate or necessary assumption if the moral world is indeed to be moral. In brief, the world as we experience it is not just, so there must be more to it than what we encounter in this life. This requires the immortality of the soul and the existence of God to mete out justice in the end. Thus, knowledge of God pertains to the sphere of practical reason.

The details of Kant's arguments do not concern us here, but rather the general form of his solution. Newtonian science (with its mechanistic conception of causality) does not contradict religious belief because it belongs to a sphere of knowledge different from the sphere to which religious knowledge belongs, and one cannot reason in any straightforward way from one sphere to the other.

Friedrich Schleiermacher adopted Kant's general strategy but argued that there are not two spheres but three: the spheres of knowing (science), doing (morality), and feeling (religion). "The piety which forms the basis of all ecclesiastical communions is, considered purely in itself, neither a Knowing nor a Doing, but a modification of Feeling, or of immediate self-consciousness."[35] So doctrines, strictly speaking, are not knowledge, but rather sys-

---

35. Schleiermacher, *The Christian Faith*, §3.

tematically ordered expressions of piety. Nor can they be derived by reasoning from any kind of knowledge.

> [Christian dogmas] are supra-rational. . . . For there is an inner experience to which they may all be traced: they rest upon a given; and apart from this they could not have arisen, by deduction or synthesis, from universally recognized and communicable propositions. . . . Therefore this supra-rationality implies that a true appropriation of Christian dogmas cannot be brought about by scientific means, and thus lies outside the realm of reason (67).

Therefore science and theology have nothing to do with one another. Adopting a term from contemporary philosophy of science, we can say that they are *incommensurable*. The drawback of this position is that science can provide no support for religious beliefs, for example, no arguments for design based on the findings of science. But the great benefit is that theology cannot conflict with the findings of science. For instance, the doctrine of creation relates to the feeling of absolute dependence in the following manner: if it were not the case that the entire universe depends on God, then, since humans are continuous with the universe, it would not be possible to say that humans depend absolutely on God. The question whether the universe began in the recent past, or billions of years ago, or whether it is eternal has no bearing on this relation of the doctrine to the experience of absolute dependence, and thus scientific accounts of the origin of the universe cannot conflict with the doctrine.

Early American liberals tended to give more attention to the compatibility of theology with science than to arguing for the distinctions between them, but in one way or another the compatibility is ensured by the compartmentalization. Shailer Mathews emphasized the need to use different patterns of speech to express the Christian faith in different eras. It does not matter if true attitudes toward God and true experience of God's presence were expressed by means of imperfect or even mistaken scientific views of the past.[36] However, modern science, especially evolutionary biology, contributes new thought patterns valuable for doctrinal expression. For example, science suggests that reality be conceived in terms of boundless *activity* and *process*. These concepts provide better analogies for thinking of God than the static, materialistic concepts of earlier days.[37]

We have already seen that for Tracy the primary way in which science and religion relate is that the very existence of science raises limit questions, for example, why is the universe comprehensible? Limit questions in turn provoke religious experience—recognition of one's basic faith in the mean-

---

36. Mathews, *The Faith of Modernism*, 51.

37. Shailer Mathews et al., *Contributions of Science to Religion* (New York: D. Appleton and Company, 1924), 402, 406-7.

ingfulness of existence—which in turn are expressed in the confessions of faith that ground theological reflection. So changes in the specific content of science do not threaten theology.

Kaufman's understanding of the relations between science and theology is complex. In earlier writings he gave attention to an understanding of divine action that is not threatened by a deterministic account of the laws of nature. We take up these issues in the next chapter. In *In Face of Mystery* he sets out to construct a theological understanding of the place of humankind in the cosmos. This understanding must be worked out in relation to a concept of God and also in relation to everything we know about the cosmos from the natural sciences and about ourselves from the human sciences.

Here again theology cannot be affected adversely by science. First, this approach to theology explicitly requires that theological concepts be revised in light of new knowledge. Second, the concept *God* is a concept of a different logical type than concepts of empirical realities; it is "on a different level." It serves an organizing function with relation to other concepts. In particular, "the monotheistic idea of one God performs" the function of "holding all value and meaning and being together in systematic structural interconnection . . . something that modern scientific conceptions and pictures have (notoriously) been unable to do" (435).

So, to sum up for Kant, religion is protected from conflict with science because these two belong to isolated realms of thought and experience. For some early American liberals there are two distinct spheres of experience, the empirical and the religious, and harmony can be achieved by appropriating scientific language for doctrinal expression.[38] In contemporary liberal theologies one wants to say somehow that religion and science pertain to different conceptual *levels* (Kaufman) or different *dimensions* of experience (Tracy). In all cases religion and science are given complementary roles in human life, which is reflected in accounts of the differences between religious and scientific languages. The complementarity divides the intellectual territory in such a way that the results of science cannot conflict with faith; the accounts of language, in extreme cases, even make dialogue between science and theology impossible.

The situation is entirely different for the conservatives. Here scientific and religious language are of exactly the same type—commensurate. In many cases the referents are different, but in some critical instances they overlap: secular history and salvation history describe the adventures of the same people; the doctrine of creation describes the origin of the same universe as

---

38. A contemporary version of this strategy is to adopt scientific terms for metaphorical use in theology. See, for example, Stephen Happel, "Metaphors and Time Asymmetry: Cosmologies in Physics and Christian Meanings," in *Quantum Cosmology and the Laws of Nature: Scientific Perspectives on Divine Action*, ed. Robert John Russell, Nancey Murphy, and C. J. Isham (Vatican City State: Vatican Observatory, 1993), 103-34.

does cosmology and geology and the same biological species as does the theory of evolution.

Augustine's metaphor of the two books of God's revelation, the Bible and nature, is commonly invoked, and so Charles Hodge states that

> As the Bible is of God, it is certain that there can be no conflict between the teachings of the Scriptures and the facts of science. It is not with the facts, but with theories, believers have to contend. Many such theories have, from time to time, been presented, apparently or really inconsistent with the Bible. But these theories have either proved to be false, or to harmonize with the Word of God, properly interpreted.[39]

Hodge believed that proper interpretation of the creation accounts in Genesis would solve apparent conflicts with geology over the age of the earth. He found textual grounds for interpreting the "days" in Genesis 1 as periods of indefinite length, and he urged that if one interpretation of the term "brings the Mosaic account into conflict with facts, and another sense avoids such conflict, then it is obligatory on us to adopt that other" (571).

Hodge was much taken with efforts of his day to harmonize the creation narratives with scientific accounts of the order of development of the cosmos, the planet, and the various forms of life, and concludes with irrepressible enthusiasm that

> there is so much that the most recent readings of science have for the first time explained, that the idea of man as the author [of the Bible] becomes utterly incomprehensible. By proving the record true, science pronounces it divine; for who could have correctly narrated the secrets of eternity but God himself?[40]

However, it is another matter with the theory of evolution. This theory *cannot* be true because it is thoroughly atheistic.

> God has revealed his existence and his government of the world so clearly and so authoritatively, that any philosophical or scientific speculations inconsistent with those truths are like cobwebs in the track of a tornado. They offer no sensible resistance.[41]

Darwin's proposal is described as mere theory or hypothesis, incapable of proof, and Hodge notes that Darwin himself recognizes counter-evidence.

It is important to remember that for all the publicity devoted to anti-evolutionists, it is not the case that all conservatives reject the theory; this

---

39. Charles Hodge, *Systematic Theology*, 1:573.
40. Ibid.; quoting James D. Dana, *Bibliotheca Sacra* (January 1856), 110.
41. Charles Hodge, *Systematic Theology*, 2:15.

was not true even among Hodge's generation. A. H. Strong was one of the early conservatives who concluded that something like Darwin's theory of the origin of species was true,[42] but this scientific account could be reconciled with the Bible by interpreting evolution as the means by which the various species were created by God (466). He notes that the Genesis text does not inform us whether "man's physical system is or is not derived by natural descent, from the lower animals" (465). However, he held that the human soul could not have evolved.

Contemporary conservatives are also divided on the question of whether the theory of evolution conflicts with Christian teaching. Many have adopted positions like Strong's, generally termed theistic evolution; others still reject the theory; and there is a variety of strategies for accommodation in between. Bloesch is one who rejects the theory. In giving an account of the distinguishing characteristics of evangelical theology he writes:

> Evangelical theology will give a qualified approval to the historical-critical method, but it will reject the naturalistic philosophy of many of the higher critics. It will display a readiness to take into account scientific discoveries and new scientific evidence, even if this calls into question certain reputed historical facts or opinions of the world and man found in the Bible. The theory of evolution is not a scientific fact, however, and therefore Evangelical theology has been basically right in its continued opposition to Darwinism and especially social Darwinism. Evangelicals will value the scientific method (though not as a pathway to knowledge of God), but they will be on the alert against scientism, the naturalist philosophy that makes use of science for its own sake.[43]

The reference to historical criticism in Bloesch's characterization of evangelical theology raises a closely related issue. The very same propositionalism that requires science and revelation to compete for the same intellectual territory creates comparable problems in relating biblical history to "scientific" history and has led to debates nearly as acrimonious. A similar range of strategies for reconciliation have been developed to deal with the results of higher criticism. Here, as in the relation with natural science, the view that Scripture and doctrine make straightforward factual claims about God's universe means that they are capable of running afoul of claims from other disciplines.[44]

---

42. Strong, *Systematic Theology*, 392.

43. Bloesch, *Essentials of Evangelical Theology, Volume One: God, Authority, and Salvation*, 16.

44. As far as I have been able to determine, McGrath has not addressed the issue of science and religion; he does, however, give attention to the problems of historical criticism. This fact may reflect a difference in the intellectual climates of Britain and the United States.

SUMMARY

In this chapter I have expanded the descriptions of two ideal types of theology, which I claim were *preordained*, in a sense, by modern philosophical options. I claimed that the experiential foundationalism and inside-out approaches to religious knowledge of the liberal type demanded an expressivist theory of religious language. Expressivism, conveniently, turned out to be one of the two options made available by modern philosophy for the understanding of language generally. I argued, further, that experiential-expressivism lends itself to justifying proposals for the feminizing of language about God; it also accounts for the fact that the liberal type of theologian takes religion and science to be incommensurable, and thus finds no possible conflicts between them.

The scriptural foundationalist, outside-in approach to religious knowledge of the conservative type makes a propositional account of religious language possible. Propositionalism, a version of the predominant representative or referential theory of modern philosophy, leads its proponents to be cautious in changing linguistic forms, since the language is being used to make precise statements about the character of God. Because the propositions of theology are commensurable with other kinds of knowledge, it also creates problems of consistency with both science and history.

3

Immanence or Intervention

How Does God Act in the World?

INTRODUCTION

In the years following Isaac Newton's formulation of the laws of mechanics, modern philosophers and scientists came to think of the universe as a gigantic machine. Perhaps the most striking proponent of this view was Pierre Simon de Laplace (1749-1827), who envisioned every atom in the universe as a component in an unfailingly precise cosmic clockwork mechanism. He was not unaware of the theological implications. There is a famous story in which Napoleon is said to have asked Laplace about the role of God in his system. Laplace replied: "I have no need of that hypothesis."

Laplace's response is but an extreme example of a problem that has plagued theologians throughout the modern period. I shall argue that a confluence of scientific and philosophical factors in the modern period created difficulties for an account of divine action. The first of these factors was the development of the concept of the *laws of nature.* The second was development of a modern form of *atomism.* This is in the first instance a scientific theory regarding the nature of matter, but the success of the scientific theory has led to a general view of reality (a metaphysical theory) to the effect that in any system the functioning of the parts accounts for the characteristics of the whole. This metaphysical thesis is a form of *reductionism.* When atomism and reductionism are combined with the assumption that deterministic laws apply in the domain of physics—the domain of the atoms— the consequence is a determinist view of the universe. That is, the laws of physics determine the behavior of the atoms and the behavior of the atoms determines the behavior of all the larger wholes of which they are a part.

Determinism presents two problems. One has to do with free will and the relationship between mind and body: if the body is nothing but an arrangement of atoms whose behavior is governed by the laws of physics, then how can free decisions affect it? The second problem is analogous: if science gives a complete and adequate account of the causes of all events, where, if at all, is there room for God to act? My thesis is that modern theologians have found only two strategies for reconciling their accounts of divine action with the Newtonian-Laplacian worldview. We shall see that liberals and conservatives divide rather neatly into two camps on this issue. Conservatives typically take an *interventionist* approach to divine action; that is, God is sovereign over the laws of nature and is able to overrule them to produce special divine acts. Liberals generally take an *immanentist* approach, emphasizing God's action in and through all natural processes.

There may be no other single factor that has such thoroughgoing consequences for theology; thus, the divide between liberals and conservatives on this issue opens a veritable chasm between their theological outlooks. We shall see that this issue is of fundamental importance in determining theologians' views on theological method and Scripture: immanentism requires an experiential foundation for theology, since Scriptural foundationalism is dependent upon an interventionist view of revelation. One's view of revelation in turn affects one's theory of religious language and the positions available regarding the relationship between science and religion.

ATOMISM, REDUCTIONISM, AND DETERMINISM

The goal of this section is to highlight a metaphysical view, a theory about the essential nature of reality, that has been implicit in the development of modern science, and has been held explicitly by some modern philosophers as well. This theory can best be understood by considering its emergence in the history of science.

The first aspect of the theory is the atomist conception of matter. Galileo (1564-1642) is thought to have had his most significant impact on Christianity through his support of the Copernican theory, but his theory of matter has been a subtler (and surely more destructive) influence in the long run. Galileo was one of the first modern scientists to reject the Aristotelian theory that all things are composed of "matter" and "form" in favor of an atomic or corpuscular theory. His early version of atomism hypothesized that all physical processes could be accounted for in terms of the properties of the atoms, namely, size, shape, and rate of motion.

The success of the system of physics developed by Isaac Newton (1642-1727) depended on taking *mass* as the essential property of atoms, and on the development of the concept of a *force*. The claim that all physical processes could be understood on the basis of mechanical interactions of particles was strikingly supported by the work of Antoine-Laurent Lavoisier (1743-1796) and John Dalton (1766-1844), who demonstrated that the phenomena of chemistry could be explained on the assumption that all material substances possessed mass and were composed of corpuscles or atoms. This was a striking triumph not only for the atomic theory of matter but also for *reductionism*, that is, the strategy of analyzing a thing into its parts and then explaining the properties or behavior of the thing in terms of the properties and behavior of the parts.

This successful reduction of chemistry to physics raised the expectation that biological processes could be explained by reducing them to chemistry, and thence to physics. There have been a series of successes here, beginning in 1828 when the synthesis of urea refuted the claim that biochemistry was essentially distinct from inorganic chemistry, and continuing in current study of the physics of self-organizing systems and their bearing on the origin of life. The philosophical question whether biology could be reduced to chemistry and physics, or whether the emergence of life required additional metaphysical explanation in terms of a "vital force," was hotly debated, but vitalism had almost disappeared by the end of the nineteenth century.

What implications does atomism, coupled with reductionism, have for understanding human nature and society? The two predominant modern answers have been: everything and nothing. Materialists have looked for the reduction of the mental and the social to biology and ultimately to physics; dualists have held that essential humanness is associated with the mind and thus is quite independent of the workings of mechanistic nature.

Thomas Hobbes (1588-1679) was an early materialist. He denied the existence of any immaterial mind or soul and maintained that ideas, sensations, and appetites were all due to motions of particles in the brain. Human action could be explained as a product of desire and aversion, a pair of opposing physical forces. Hobbes understood "civil philosophy" as the study of the motions of individuals in the commonwealth. His use of the concept of the social contract to argue for absolute sovereignty is predicated on the balance of quasi-physical forces: individuals' inherent tendencies to assert themselves in quests of power need to be balanced by a counter-force, the fear of capital punishment.

The modern dualist account of human reality can be traced to Hobbes's contemporary, René Descartes. Descartes contributed significantly to the philosophical foundations of modern scientific atomism but argued that material substance was only part of reality. The other basic metaphysical principle was thinking substance. Human bodies were complex machines but the person—the 'I'—is the mind, which is entirely free.

From dualist roots in Descartes's philosophy the distinction between the natural sciences and the *Geisteswissenschaften* (the social sciences and humanities) has grown. One strong tradition throughout the modern period has claimed that these are two radically different kinds of sciences, with different methodologies, one dealing with a mechanistically conceived physical nature, the other dealing with the inner life of the mind and mind's cultural products. An equally strong tradition, well represented in the logical positivists' twentieth-century program for the unification of science, added psychology and the social sciences as upper levels to the hierarchy of the natural sciences and assumed that great progress in these fields would come about as a result of reduction of the social to the level of individual psychology, and of psychology to biology. This debate over the reducibility of the human sciences continues in contemporary philosophy of the social sciences. Methodological individualists say that social events are the product of aggregates of the actions of individuals, while methodological collectivists claim that social wholes obey their own, nonreducible social laws; naturalists hold that social science should aim to reproduce the methodological features of the natural sciences, while anti-naturalists claim that their subject matter calls for a different methodology.[1]

The debate over dualism aside, the general tendency of modern science increasingly has been to see the natural world as a total system and to conceive of it in terms of a hierarchy of levels of complexity, from the smallest sub-particles through atoms, molecules, tissues, cells, organs, organisms, societies, to ecosystems—and with the human body, if not the whole person, a part of that hierarchical system.

Causation in this view is "bottom-up"; that is, the parts of an entity are located one rung down in the hierarchy of complexity, and it is the parts that determine the characteristics of the whole, not the other way around. So ultimate causal explanations are thought to be based on laws pertaining to lower levels of the hierarchy.

Thus, there is a variety of reductionist theses, all intimately related. Ontological or metaphysical reductionism holds that higher-level entities are nothing but complex organizations of simpler entities; it is opposed to vitalism and mind-body dualism. Causal reductionism holds that ultimate causes (at least in the physical universe) are bottom-up. Methodological reductionism holds that the proper approach to scientific investigation is analysis of entities in their parts, and that the laws governing the behavior of higher-level entities should be reducible to (shown to be special instances of) the laws of the lower levels. The success of methodological reductionism in modern science is what lends credence to the two other sorts of reductionism.

The crucial metaphysical assumption is that the parts of an entity or system determine the character and behavior of the whole, and not vice versa. This is metaphysical atomism-reductionism. The thesis is much broader than the atomic theory of matter in science and pervades a variety of areas of thought. For example, modern ethics assumes an individualist account of human good; the common good is simply a summation of goods for individuals. Modern philosophy of language is largely atomistic in assuming that the meaning of discourse is a function of the meanings of the relevant parts. The logical positivists, quintessential modern thinkers, sought to identify the atomic

---

1. Karl Popper has been one of the most noted recent proponents of individualism and naturalism. Charles Taylor is one of the best-known contemporary advocates of anti-naturalism.

facts that would serve as the ultimate foundation for the whole scientific edifice.

DETERMINISM AND THE MIND-BODY PROBLEM

If we add to the atomist-reductionist assumptions of modernity the further assumption that the laws of physics are deterministic, the result is that it is nearly impossible (or perhaps entirely impossible) to avoid the conclusion that all processes in the physical universe are strictly determined—we have Laplace's vision of a world in which each event is preordained by a combination of initial conditions and natural laws.

As we have seen, some have been willing to accept the determinist consequences for human nature. For example, Hobbes claimed that human actions were all determined by the motions of matter in the brain; nevertheless, those actions that were determined solely by these internal factors, and not constrained by external forces, could still be called "free."

The goal of protecting human freedom from determinism has been a primary motivation for dualism. In addition to Cartesian mind-body dualism, there was also Immanuel Kant's strategy of distinguishing the phenomenal realm—the realm of sensory reality, where Newton's laws apply—from *noumena*, things-in-themselves, which include God and human selves. However, it is now widely recognized that dualism has not solved the problem of determinism because of the dualists' inability to give a satisfactory account of how a free but *immaterial* mind (or a noumenal self) could have any causal interaction with the physical world. In particular, there is the problem of how a decision or act of will could cause a bodily action. The problem is twofold: One aspect is that if the mind is a causal agent, then any bodily event it effects is over-determined. Suppose that a mental event, M, causes a brain event, B. Whatever the nature of B, it will have been the case that B was preceded by a series of other brain events. The brain events are, according to the determinist view, connected in a law-like manner. How does the mental event insert itself into this otherwise lawfully governed sequence of physical events?

Second, in a physical world where nothing happens except by means of a force, an expenditure of energy, how can a nonmaterial mind have an effect? One answer would be to think in terms of something like psychic energy, but this is to misunderstand the modern conception of mind; that is, it makes mind simply a part of the complex of matter and forces. Such a "mind force," if it were effective, would necessarily be measurable, and no such thing has been discovered. In addition to raising this empirical problem, the psychic-energy theory defeats the purpose of exempting mind from the system of natural laws in the first place, especially from the law of the conservation of matter and energy.

Recognition of these difficulties, and the judgment that they are insuper-able, has driven most contemporary philosophers to reject mind-body dual-ism.

THE PROBLEM OF DIVINE ACTION

In the medieval period, especially after the integration of the lost works of Aristotle into Western thought, God's action in the world could be explained in a way perfectly consistent with the scientific knowledge of the time. Heaven was part of the "physical" cosmos. God's agents, the angels, controlled the movements of the "seven planets," which in turn gave nature its rhythms. But modern science has changed all that, primarily by its dependence on the concept of the laws of nature. The notion of a law of nature began as a metaphorical extension of the idea of a divinely sanctioned moral code.[2] For early modern scientists, as well as for medieval theologians, the laws of nature provided an account of how God managed the physical universe. In fact, Descartes took the laws of motion to follow from a more basic prin-ciple, explicitly theological: "God is the First Cause of movement and . . . always preserves an equal amount of movement in the universe."[3]

However, after a century or so the metaphorical character of the term *law of nature* had been forgotten. The laws were granted some form of real existence independent of God, and it is one of the ironies of history that they later came even to be seen as obstacles to divine purposes. Whereas for Newton a complete account of the motions of the solar system had required both the divinely willed laws of motion and God's constant readjustment, for Laplace it was no longer necessary for God to make adjustments and, finally, the question was raised whether it was even *conceivable* that God should intervene.

Had the problem of God's governance only concerned astronomical pre-dictions and calculations it would have been of no great concern to theolo-gians. However, reductionism and the conception of the hierarchical order-ing of the systems in the universe meant that the problem of divine action relates to all sorts of (physical) processes.

The problem is parallel to the problem of mind-body interaction. First, if God acts, this requires that God violate, override, or suspend the laws of nature, which otherwise would have brought about some different event. Many have argued that this is an unacceptable view of the nature of God. If God created the laws in the first place, then God's violation of them is irra-

---

2. See Bas C. van Fraassen, *Laws and Symmetry* (Oxford: Clarendon Press, 1989), 1-14.

3. René Descartes, *Principles of Philosophy* (1644), part II, xxxvi.

tional; the Jewish philosopher Baruch Spinoza (1632-1677) argued that in such a case God would be involved in self-contradiction.

Second, if action in the material world requires a force, then to conceive of God making things happen in the world is to conceive of God as a force among forces. This, too, is theologically problematic, since it reduces God to the level of a demiurge.

The simplest reconciliation of divine action with the modern conception of the clockwork universe was Deism, a very popular option in the eighteenth century. The Deists, whose number in America included Thomas Jefferson and Benjamin Franklin, concluded that while God was the creator of the universe and author of the laws of nature, God was not at all involved in ongoing natural processes or in human affairs. They maintained a notion of God as the source of moral principles, but the most extreme rejected all the rest of positive religion, including the notion of revelation.

The thesis of this chapter is that for those who would stay within the Christian fold, there have been but two options, here labeled *interventionism* and *immanentism*.

INTERVENTIONISM

Interventionism has generally been the doctrine of choice for conservative theologians. These theologians hold that in addition to God's creative activity, which includes ordaining the laws of nature, God occasionally violates or suspends those very laws in order to bring about an extraordinary event. God makes something happen that would not have happened in the ordinary course of nature. According to Charles Hodge, there are three classes of events when regarded from the perspective of divine action:

> In the first place, there are events . . . due to the ordinary operations of second causes, as upheld and guided by God. To this class belong the common processes of nature; the growth of plants and animals, the orderly movements of the heavenly bodies; and the more unusual occurrences, earthquakes, volcanic eruptions, and violent agitations and revolutions in human societies. In the second place, there are events due to the influences of the Holy Spirit upon the hearts of men, such as regeneration, sanctification, spiritual illumination, etc. Thirdly, there are events which belong to neither of these classes, and whose distinguishing characteristics are, First, that they take place in the external world, *i.e.*, in the sphere of the observation of the senses; and Secondly, that they are produced or caused by the simple volition of God, without the intervention of any subordinate cause. To this class belongs the original act of creation, in which all cooperation of second causes was impossible. To the same class belong all events truly mi-

raculous. A miracle, therefore, may be defined to be an event, in the external world, brought about by the immediate efficiency, or simple volition of God.[4]

In response to the question of how God relates to the laws of nature, Hodge writes:

> The answer to that question, as drawn from the Bible is, First, that He is their author. He endowed matter with these forces, and ordained that they should be uniform. Secondly, He is independent of them. He can change, annihilate, or suspend them at pleasure. He can operate with them or without them. "The Reign of Law" must not be made to extend over Him who made the laws. Thirdly, as the stability of the universe, and the welfare, and even the existence of organized creatures, depend on the uniformity of the laws of nature, God never does disregard them except for the accomplishment of some high purpose. He, in the ordinary operations of his Providence, operates with and through the laws which He has ordained. He governs the material, as well as the moral world by law (1:607).

So it is a mistake to think that the laws, once "created," are immutable; they merely reflect God's ordinary way of working, which God is able and willing to suspend upon occasion for some higher purpose.

Note that the assumption held by some contemporary Christians that an event is an act of God only if it cannot be explained by natural laws is, by Hodge's standards, a degenerate view of divine action. God works in the regular processes just as much as in miraculous interventions. Much of the controversy over evolution would dissolve if it were not assumed by many conservatives that scientific accounts and accounts of divine creative action are mutually exclusive.

A significant difference between Hodge's position in 1891 and Donald Bloesch's in 1994 is a greater sensitivity to the fact that the modern theologian's problem of divine action is historically situated. This is seen, for example, in Bloesch's criticism of Rudolf Bultmann:

> Part of the problem is that Bultmann denied the possibility of divine intervention into nature and history. He accepted uncritically the presuppositions of Newtonian science, which portray the phenomenal world as a closed continuum of cause and effect. Explanation must consequently be couched in terms of modern ideas of causation. For Bultmann, the "natural" course of events is *never* interrupted; the cata-

---

4. Charles Hodge, *Systematic Theology*, 1:618.

clysmic is therefore routinely disregarded. His commitment to both uniformitarianism and historicism definitely clouded his understanding not only of myth but of the kerygma itself.[5]

Bloesch makes a similar point regarding contemporary higher criticism of the Bible:

> We should resist the naturalistic presuppositions that higher critics bring to the text and thereby distort its real meaning. As critics of the critics we must reject uniformitarianism—that everything happens within a closed order of cause and effect. In this view miracles understood as divine interventions in history cannot happen. We must also repudiate historical and cultural determinism—that an investigation into their historical and cultural milieu can *wholly* account for the ideas expressed in the Bible (267).

This critique of the presuppositions of uniformitarianism and determinism leaves Bloesch free, as he sees it, to emphasize God's action in history: The Bible is a description of God's mighty acts (263). The angel of God really did bring down the Assyrians (265). The bodily resurrection of Christ was a historical event (267).

Another contemporary evangelical theologian, more conservative than Bloesch, is interesting for the way he meets head on the problem of reconciling God's activity with scientific views of natural *forces*. Millard Erickson defines miracles as "those special supernatural works of God's providence which are not explicable on the basis of the usual patterns of nature." However, he says: "One of the important issues regarding miracles involves their relationship to natural laws or the laws of nature."[6] Erickson considers several proposed answers, including the view that miracles require that the laws of nature be broken. His preferred position is the following:

> A third conception is the idea that when miracles occur, natural forces are countered by supernatural force. In this view, the laws of nature are not suspended. They continue to operate, but supernatural force is introduced, negating the effect of the natural law. [Here Erickson refers to C. S. Lewis's book *Miracles*.] In the case of the [floating] axhead [recorded in 2 Kings 6:6], for instance, the law of gravity continued to function in the vicinity of the axhead, but the unseen hand of God was underneath it, bearing it up, just as if a human hand were lifting it. This view has the advantage of regarding miracles as being genuinely

---

5. Bloesch, *Holy Scripture*, 237.

6. Millard Erickson, *Christian Theology*, one-volume ed. (Grand Rapids, MI: Baker, 1983); quotations from seventh edition, 406.

supernatural or extranatural, but without being antinatural, as the second view makes them to be. To be sure, in the case of the [great catch of] fish, it may have been the conditions in the water which caused the fish to be there, but those conditions would not have been present if God had not influenced such factors as the water flow and temperature. And at times there may have been acts of creation as well, as in the case of the feeding of the five thousand (408).

So Bloesch calls into question the assumption of the law-governed character of the universe but provides no alternative to the modern account. Erickson explicitly makes God a force among forces, and illustrates well the position that the liberals are at pains to avoid.

IMMANENTISM

The liberals' immanentist view of divine action was a reaction both against Deism, with its view that God is not active at all within the created world, and against the conservative theologians' view that God performs special, miraculous acts. The liberal view emphasizes the universal presence of God in the world and God's continual, creative, and purposive activity in and through all the processes of nature and history.[7] This view made it possible to understand progress, both evolutionary progress in the natural world and human progress in society, as manifestations of God's purposes.

A primary motive for emphasizing God's action *within* natural processes was the acceptance of the modern scientific view of the world as a closed system of natural causes, along with the judgment that a view of divine activity as intervention reflected an inferior grasp of God's intelligence and power. That is, it suggested that God was unable to achieve all of the divine purposes through an original ordering, and also that God was inconsistent in willing laws and then also willing their violation. In short, the higher view of divine action was thought to be one in which God did not need to intervene. Thus, the interpretation of divine activity in terms of miracles tended to disappear in the liberal tradition.

We find variations on these themes from Schleiermacher up through the present. Schleiermacher claimed that divine providence and the operation of causal laws entirely coincide, and that the word *miracle* is just the religious word for *event*. Furthermore, he argued that it can never be in the best interest of religion to interpret an event as a special act of God in opposition to its being a part of the system of nature, since so to interpret it works against the sense of the absolute dependence of the *whole* upon God.[8]

---

7. See Owen Thomas, ed., *God's Activity in the World: The Contemporary Problem* (Chico, CA: Scholars Press, 1983), 3.

8. Schleieirmacher, *The Christian Faith*, §§46 and 47.

Shailer Mathews asks if we can still believe in "God the Father almighty, maker of heaven and earth" in the face of the uniformity of nature. Mathews takes Deism to be an attempted solution to the problem of divine action inspired by the political events of the early modern period.

> Englishmen who lived during the latter part of the seventeenth century and shared in the establishment of the constitutional monarchy which replaced the Stuarts, thought of God as in a way transferring his immediate control of nature to laws, something as kings transferred some of their prerogatives to Parliament. But Deism could not long endure.[9]

Thus, God's relation to the universe must be expressed in new ways suited to new discoveries:

> Our knowledge of the universe with its laws and processes, is making us more certain that reason and purpose are immanent within its infinite activity. Matter itself has ceased to be dead, and has become vibrant with activity, instinct with order. The consensus of investigators that there is within nature a process which is evolutionary, forces us to the conviction that there must be that which is personal in that from which human personality has emerged (108).

True to type, Mathews believes that this immanentist account of God's action rules out miracles:

> Is belief in the existence and providence of God dependent upon the belief in super- or contra-naturalism? Must we think of God's presence in the world only in terms used by miracle-believing minds? There can be no question as to the answer which will be given by men who have been so convinced by the evidence presented by scientific research as to feel the supremacy of law and process in the natural order. To such minds, miracle in any real sense of the word, is unthinkable. The world-view on which it rests has vanished. But there is something vastly more reassuring for faith in God in our scientific knowledge of cosmos and law, of forces of matter and of the successive, ever more personal stages of life. Indeed, one might almost say that the evidence of God's presence in our world rests upon the precisely opposite argument from that upon which it rested in the minds of the past. It is the unity of cosmic order, discoverable law and evolution that argue the divine

---

9. Mathews, *The Faith of Modernism*, 106. Notice that this is an excellent illustration of Mathews's claim (described in Chapter 2) that doctrines express religious attitudes in "patterns" appropriate to the age, especially patterns drawn from political life.

presence rather than some inexplicable violation of accustomed experience (112-13).

Gordon Kaufman expresses the seriousness of the problem of divine action, saying that unless it can be resolved "we are condemned either to live in an intolerable tension between our religious language and life and the rest of experience . . . or to give up Christian faith and talk as outmoded and no longer relevant to the actual structures of our lives and the world."[10]
Kaufman claims that particular acts of God performed from time to time .in history and nature are not just improbable or difficult to believe, but "literally inconceivable" (148). For this reason, if we are to understand the phrase "act of God," we should use it to designate the "master act" in which God is involved, namely, the whole course of history. God's action consists in giving the world its structure and giving history its direction.
This concept of divine action provides a more austere account of providence than is often found in Christian circles:

> This is no God who "walks with me and talks with me" in close interpersonal communion, giving his full attention to my complaints, miraculously extracting me from difficulties into which I have gotten myself by invading nature and history with *ad hoc* rescue operations from on high (156).

Instead, the paradigm of divine action is the story of a man praying that this cup might pass from him, "that prayer answered not with legions of angels to rescue him but with lonely suffering on a cross"; but this is followed by the birth of faith and hope in a new community after his death.

> The God who works in this fashion to turn the darkest despairs and defeats into further steps toward the realization of his beneficent ultimate objectives, without violently ripping into the fabric of history or arbitrarily upsetting the momentum of its powers, is one who can also be conceived as working within and through the closely textured natural and historical processes of our modern experience: this is a God who acts, a living God, the adequate object for a profound faith, and his action is not completely unintelligible to a mind instructed and informed by modern science and history (157).

Kaufman's language gives evidence of a measure of scorn for Christians with more robust views of divine action, and also a sense (somewhat sur-

---

10. Gordon Kaufman, "On the Meaning of 'Act of God,'" *Harvard Theological Review* 61 (1968): 175-201. Reprinted in Thomas, *God's Activity in the World: The Contemporary Problem*, 137-61; page references are to the reprint; quotation, 153.

prising for a pacifist) that God's involvement in particular events could only be violent.

A. H. STRONG ON DIVINE ACTION

Strong merits special attention for the several ways in which he fails to conform to type. In the previous chapters he has served as a representative of early conservative theology, and in some ways his position on divine action is consistent with that of other conservative theologians. He speaks of Scripture as the record of "supernatural events and communications,"[11] and emphasizes (as did Locke and his followers) that the revelatory status of Scripture is attested by miracles.

However, with the liberals he emphasizes that God works immanently in nature. He rejects the concept of miracle as a violation of the laws of nature and provides an alternative definition:

> A miracle is an event in nature, so extraordinary in itself and so coinciding with the prophecy or command of a religious teacher or leader, as fully to warrant the conviction, on the part of those who witness it, that God has wrought it with the design of certifying that this teacher or leader has been commissioned by him.
>
> This definition has certain marked advantages as compared with the preliminary definition given above: —(a) It recognizes the immanence of God and his immediate agency in nature, instead of assuming an antithesis between the laws of nature and the will of God. (b) It regards the miracle as simply an extraordinary act of that same God who is already present in all natural operations and who in them is revealing his general plan. (c) It holds that natural law, as the method of God's regular activity, in no way precludes unique exertions of this power when these will best secure his purpose in creation. (d) It leaves it possible that all miracles may have their natural explanations and may hereafter be traced to natural causes, while both miracles and their natural causes may be only names for the one and self-same will of God. (e) It reconciles the claims of both science and religion: of science, by permitting any possible or probable physical antecedents of the miracle; of religion, by maintaining that these very antecedents together with the miracle itself are to be interpreted as signs of God's special commission to him under whose teaching or leadership the miracle is wrought (118-19).

So Strong's position is that God works immanently rather than in an interventionist manner, and yet there are special (miraculous) events as well.

---

11. Strong, *Systematic Theology*, 27.

This would seem to falsify the thesis that modern assumptions allow for two and only two positions on divine action. However, I claim that Strong is in fact an exception that proves the rule.[12] In his own context he appears simply to be inconsistent, affirming "supernatural events" but also claiming that "all miracles may have their natural explanations."

However, the modern problem of divine action is a consequence of the modern reductionist, bottom-up account of causation. Strong comes very close to enunciating what I shall describe in Chapter 6 as a postmodern, "top-down" account of causation. That is, he recognizes that agents at a higher level of the hierarchy of complexity can use lower-level regularities to enact their intentions without violating those lower-level laws. He says:

> An event in nature may be caused by an agent in nature yet above nature. This is evident from the following considerations:
>
> (a) Lower forces and laws in nature are frequently counteracted and transcended by the higher (as mechanical forces and laws by chemical, and chemical by vital), while yet the lower forces and laws are not suspended or annihilated, but are merged in the higher, and made to assist in accomplishing purposes to which they are altogether unequal when left to themselves. . . .
>
> (b) The human will acts upon its physical organism, and so upon nature, and produces results which nature left to herself never could accomplish, while yet no law of nature is suspended or violated. Gravitation still operates upon the axe, even while man holds it at the surface of the water—for the axe still has weight (cf. 2 Kings 6:5-7) (121).

The question, now, is how to avoid Erickson's move of making God into a force, a "hidden hand." Strong does make statements that sound very much like Erickson's:

> What the human will, considered as a supernatural force, and what the chemical and vital forces of nature itself, are demonstrably able to accomplish, cannot be regarded as beyond the power of God, so long as God dwells in and controls the universe. If man's will can act directly upon matter in his own physical organism, God's will can work immediately upon the system which he has created and which he sustains. In other words, if there be a God, and if he be a personal being, miracles are possible (122).

---

12. "Proves the rule" in the sense that cases first appearing to falsify a generalization are shown to be "outside of . . . the principle they seem to contradict," and thus give us greater confidence in the rule. See *Fowler's Modern English Usage*, 2d ed. (Oxford: Oxford University Press, 1983), s.v. "exception."

Strong intends to avoid the objectionable aspects of interventionism by emphasizing God's immanence. It is not that God's action itself is a force among forces in the universe, but rather that God's will directs the forces of the universe, bringing about higher levels of reality and also extraordinary events.

> Evolution, then, depends on increments of force *plus* continuity of plan. New creations are possible because the immanent God has not exhausted himself. Miracle is possible because God is not far away, but is at hand to do whatever the needs of his moral universe may require. . . . If we were deists, believing in a distant God and a mechanical universe, evolution and Christianity would be irreconcilable. But since we believe in a dynamical universe, of which the personal and living God is the inner source of energy, evolution is but the basis, foundation and background of Christianity, the silent and regular working of him who, in the fulness of time, utters his voice in Christ and the Cross (123).

We shall have to consider in Chapter 6 whether a view similar to Strong's does avoid all of the problems associated with divine action in the modern period. The point here is that if Strong has succeeded in holding together a respect for the integrity of nature with a robust sense of special divine acts, he has done so by denying the reductionist assumptions of modernity.

THE PERVASIVE INFLUENCE OF THEORIES OF DIVINE ACTION

I want to draw some connections between this chapter and the topics of its predecessors. Here we have examined theories of divine action; Chapter 2 considered views of religious language and related views of the relationship between religion and science; Chapter 1 examined theological method and related views of epistemology. What I want to argue now is that a theologian's position on divine action will call for one or another approach to theological method, religious language, and the relationship between religion and science.

Recall that the foundationalist model of knowledge called for indubitable beliefs as a starting point for theology. Modern (Protestant) theologians have found only two possible sources for such beliefs: Scripture or a peculiar sort of universal religious experience. A theory of religious language correlates with each of these starting points: Representationalism or propositionalism is supported by the view that God has revealed in Scripture information about unseen realities. The expressivist view—that religious language at its most basic is a symbolic expression of the believer's religious awareness—is a correlative of experiential foundationalism, since both assume that the essence of religion is an inward awareness of God. The propositionalist view of religion makes it susceptible to conflict with science; the expressivist view protects it from such conflict.

The connections with the topic of divine action are as follows: If one holds an interventionist view of divine action, then it is perfectly reasonable to expect God to intervene in the world of human thought. In other words, the revelation contained in Scripture is but one (very important) instance among many of direct, providential action by God on our behalf. In short, Scripture itself is a miracle, understood in interventionist terms.

Archibald Alexander Hodge makes this connection clear. To the question "What are the necessary presuppositions . . . , which must be admitted before the possibility of inspiration . . . can be affirmed?" he answers: first, "the existence of a personal God, possessing the attributes of power, intelligence, and moral excellence in absolute perfection," and, second, "that in his relation to the universe he is at once immanent and transcendent. Above all, and freely acting upon all from without. Within all, and acting through the whole and every part from within, in the exercise of all his perfections, and according to the laws and modes of action he has established for his creatures, sustaining and governing them, and all their actions."[13] So Hodge is claiming that God's immanent action must be supplemented by action from without if there is to be a revelation.

Strong puts it more simply: "Religious ideas do not spring up wholly from within. External revelation can impart them. Man can reveal himself to man by external communication, and, if God has equal power with man, God can reveal himself to man in like manner."[14] This quotation nicely illustrates the outside-in character of conservative epistemology as well.

Hodge goes on to assert that the divine influence by which God's self-revelation is accomplished extends even to the choice of words, so that the thoughts God intended to convey are communicated with infallible accuracy.[15] So here we see Hodge's foundationalism wedded to an extreme form of the representationalist theory of language and both grounded in his interventionist view of God's action. With such a source of theological knowledge, who would want to turn to the nebulous realm of religious experience as a source for theology, or allow one's theology to be corrected by the fallible results of science?

Maurice Wiles is a contemporary theologian whose position on divine action is quite similar to Kaufman's in emphasizing that God enacts the whole of history but does not perform any special divine acts. Wiles recognizes the connection between theories of divine action and the proper use of Scripture in theology:

---

13. A. A. Hodge, *Outlines of Theology*, 65.
14. Strong, *Systematic Theology*, 12.
15. A. A. Hodge, *Outlines of Theology*, 66-67.

If we agree that the acceptance of some authority . . . [such as the Bible] . . . is a part of the tradition within which a Christian theologian works, we shall have to acknowledge that when we take up the question of divine action, of what we can properly mean by speaking of God acting, we appear to be deeply committed already on the subject of our investigation. . . . For whatever may be our precise conception of the inspiration of the prophets or biblical writers . . . it has normally been understood to involve some kind of special divine action. . . . Unless God acts in a special way in special events it is difficult to see how we could have religious authorities from within history and with the degree of specialness which Christians do in fact ascribe to their authorities.[16]

However, the purpose of Wiles's article is to argue that one can nonetheless attribute some authority to Scripture *without* an interventionist account of divine action. His strategy is to claim that while God acts uniformly in all events, some people respond more fully to God's presence and their words provide authoritative guidance for others. Wiles puts it as follows:

Now it is an inevitable feature of the variety to be found within human history that some people by virtue of their personality and of their situation are more fully responsive to the divine action than others. Their words and actions in turn will provide a particularly important focus for calling out such responses from others who follow them. And since that quality of life in them to which others will respond was itself grounded in responsiveness to the divine action, we may rightly speak of the events of their lives as acts of God in a special sense towards those of us who are influenced by them. In calling them special acts of God we would not be implying that there was any fundamental difference in the relation of the divine action to the particular worldly occurrences of their situation; we would be referring to the depth of response and the creative potential for eliciting further response from others embodied in those particular lives or those particular events (188).

The most important such life, for Christians, of course, is that of Jesus Christ. Thus, Wiles continues:

If certain events [such as the life of Jesus] can be given such special importance without implying a different kind of activity on God's part in relation to the worldly occurrences concerned, then clearly the records

---

16. Maurice Wiles, "Religious Authority and Divine Action," in Thomas, *God's Activity in the World*, 181-94; quotation, 181-82.

which partly record and partly constitute such events can properly be regarded as having religious authority without that fact implying any special interventionist activity as responsible either for their composition or for their recognition as authoritative (191-92).

So Wiles is confident that an immanentist account of divine action is compatible with granting the Scriptures the status of "a religious authority of the utmost importance" (193). However, such a view allows one to ascribe some measure of religious authority to the scriptures of other faiths, as well. Here Wiles's position is similar to Tracy's claim that the Christian Scriptures are best understood as classics and thus members of a large class of works that express "events of understanding."

Wiles suggests that some particular teachings in the Christian Scriptures can be rejected on the grounds that they conflict with more important scriptural doctrines. So it is clear that while Wiles is able to justify a special place for Scripture on the basis of his immanentist account of divine action, he is not able to justify a *foundationalist* use of Scripture. Religious experience, understood by Wiles in terms of greater responsiveness to God's action within the world, is the more basic category.

Strong's phrase, quoted above, about religious ideas springing up from within the person is an apt account of the liberal view of inspiration. Since God does not directly impart knowledge of religious realities, this knowledge must arise within human consciousness by natural means—an inside-out approach—by perception of the divine dimension within or under surface realities; revelatory events are "events of understanding." A common way of putting the matter in contemporary language is to say that religion involves the perception of the meaning of reality as opposed to mere knowledge of the facts.

As mentioned in Chapter 2, there is a connection between experiential foundationalism and the expressivist theory of religious language. The religious experience that is the source of theology—perception of religious meanings—does not come with precise descriptions attached. The human race must grope for adequate expression. The appropriate kind of language is symbolic or metaphorical. It aims at expressing the inner feelings, religious attitudes, or existential orientation of the speaker. It is not, in any straightforward sense, a representation of objective realities and thus cannot contradict science in any way.

So the rejection of special divine acts accounts for much of the character of liberal theology, just as the interventionist view accounts for the character of conservative theology.

It is time for another summary. I have claimed that modern philosophical assumptions have created limited options for theologians, and that the choice of one option from any pair conditions one's choices elsewhere. Since choices in one area are correlated with choices in the others, we find two clear-cut patterns or types, one of which has been prevalent among liberal theologians, and the other among modern conservatives. The options are summarized in Table 2.

	Liberal	*Conservative*
knowledge	experiential foundationalism inside-out	scriptural foundationalism outside-in
language	expressivism	propositionalism
relationship with science	incommensurability	commensurability
divine action	immanentism	interventionism

Table 2.

Numerous theologians, of course, have attempted to find compromise positions between the two types, but it has been the burden of these three chapters to show that there really is no self-consistent middle ground. Thus, we find Christianity bifurcated into two distinct traditions in the modern period. From their writings (especially those of the liberals) it even appears that some theologians are unaware of the existence of the competing tradition.

SUMMARY

Here we stand at the end of the modern period. Theologians have had two hundred years to try the various permutations on each of these positions. They have elaborated theological stances within rationalist settings and romanticist settings; in terms of Continental thought and Anglo-American thought; in times of cultural optimism and dark despair. Have we reached a time in history when it is fair to say that neither of these two theological strategies will work? I cannot prove that a theological genius will not come along in the next generation to solve problems her predecessors failed to solve. But I can point out that each of the theological types just described has problems that appear at this point to be insoluble.

The problem with the foundationalist use of Scripture is the question that always arises about how one can know, with the requisite certitude, that the Christian Bible is, in fact, the revealed word of God. Conservative theologians provide arguments, but none of them is strong enough to serve as the *foundation* for a system of religion.[17]

---

17. Cf. David Hume: "We may establish as a maxim, that no human testimony can have such force as to prove a miracle, and make it a just foundation for any such system of religion." "Of Miracles," in *An Enquiry Concerning Human Understanding* (1748), part II.

There is a different but equally perplexing problem for those who attempt to use religious experience as the foundation for theology. As Wallace Matson has pointed out, all inside-out approaches to knowledge require that one argue from the inner ideas or experiences to knowledge about realities outside the mind. Such arguments have always turned out to be problematic. The liberal use of religious experience as a foundation for theology raises the question how to know that one's religious experience is experience of a real, objective divinity. That is, how can we ever know that religion is anything more than a symbolic expression of humankind's highest aspirations or basic life attitudes, as Ludwig Feuerbach had already suggested soon after Schleiermacher's day?

The problem with an interventionist account of divine action, especially of the sort expressed by Erickson, is that it does seem to neglect the qualitative difference between God's action and ordinary created causes. To make God a force that moves physical objects seems to make God a part of the system of physical forces. And if God is such a force, we ought to be able to measure divine action just as we do the forces of nature.

The problem with an immanentist view of divine action is that it either removes the aspect of intention from God's acts altogether, or else makes every event equally intentional—devastating earthquakes and the Holocaust as well as the growth of crops and the birth of Jesus.

Both accounts of religious language are defective. On the one hand, the representative or propositional view of religious language needs to be criticized for its neglect of the self-involving character of religious discourse. Also, if the just-mentioned problems with scriptural foundationalism cannot be solved, then how is one ever to know that theological propositions accurately describe a reality beyond human experience?

On the other hand, the expressivist account of religious language seems to require a sharper separation between the cognitive and the expressive functions of language than can really be maintained. Suppose we say that the doctrine of creation is not a description of something God did at the beginning of time, but rather an expression of one's sense of dependence upon God. What then is the significance of such a sense of dependence if one is not actually dependent upon God? Traditional accounts of dependence have focused on the fact that God created everything in the beginning and that God now keeps all things in existence. But if theology is not capable of making either of these statements about what God does, and of understanding them in a fairly straightforward propositional way, then what meaning does the expressivist account of the doctrine of creation have, apart from describing an inner state of the speaker? And should that inner state be of interest to anyone else?

The incommensurabilist view that religion and science are too unlike to conflict seems to disregard the point just made, that we cannot detach "meanings" from the way things are. Furthermore, it makes religion immune to attack from science, but at the cost of making religion irrelevant to a science-minded culture. The commensurabilist view seems to disregard some important differences between the purposes of religion and of science, and it disregards some important differences in the kinds of language that are used in each.

If this survey of the besetting problems of the standard modern positions in theology sounds like bad news, the good news is that all of the philosophical positions that have so limited theological options have themselves run into insurmountable obstacles and new positions have been proposed in their place. It is to these changes that we turn in the next three chapters.

Part II

4

Epistemological Holism
and Theological Method

INTRODUCTION

The fate of modern theism is the story of a traditional mode of thought and practice frustrated in its search for an acceptable response to [the] modern situation.

It is symptomatic of the state of academic theology that . . . critical essays . . . are among the most enduring theological accomplishments in recent years. Contemporary theology, like an empty pile in solitaire, is waiting for a new king to come along and get things started again.[1]

So says Jeffrey Stout. Stout is pessimistic about the appearance of such a king, and I am too. But what Stout fails to consider—and what will be the focus of the second part of this book—is the possibility that the rules of the game might be changed instead. If all the possible moves have been tried within the limits set by modernity, this should be a cause for dismay only if we believe modern thinkers have had the final word on the topics of knowledge, language, and the ultimate nature of reality. It is becoming more and more widely accepted that modern thinkers have *not* had the last word. We must now ask about the new plays that might be possible under the "rules" of the next major philosophical era.

In the first part of this book I explained what I take to be some of the most important features of modern thought in order to examine the consequences of those features for theology. I claimed that modern philosophy has been largely responsible for bifurcating Christian theology into two camps, the liberal and the conservative.

This part will provide a sampler of new *post*modern positions—theories of knowledge, language, and causation that have grown out of criticism of their modern predecessors. It will also sketch some outlines of what theol-

---

1. Stout, *The Flight from Authority*, 149, 148.

ogy might look like if it makes use of these resources. Such a theology will allow for a range of variations, some more appealing to the theological left or theological right, but there should no longer be a deep gulf between liberals and conservatives.

In particular, this chapter considers the new holist epistemology and the possibilities it opens up for new accounts of theological method. Chapter 5 examines new theories of language and their implications for understanding religious and theological language. Chapter 6 surveys changes in understandings of science that have deep metaphysical implications and thus consequences for an account of divine action as well.

POSTMODERNITY

Stephen Toulmin describes a growing sense of *discontinuity* among people in a variety of fields. We are now at the end of an era, he says, not just in the calendrical sense—the end of a millennium whose dates begin with the numeral "1," but in a deeper historical sense. We are living at the end of the historical period called modern.

Note how the very meaning of the word *modern* has shifted. It used to be a congratulatory term meaning "up to date." But now we have enough distance from the intellectual-cultural project of the past three hundred years to see its predominant features, to seek its reasons for being, to evaluate it critically. In so doing, we can imagine a new and different world.[2]

Before I begin my account of postmodern philosophy, however, I need to make some distinctions; I need to say what I do *not* mean to label postmodern. First, in the previous chapters I have presented a one-sided account of modern philosophy. While it certainly is the case that many modern philosophers can be characterized by their assent to the positions I have described, others can be characterized by reactions against these positive developments, but in ways that share the assumptions of their opponents. For example, David Hume's skeptical attack on Cartesian foundationalism was as committed to foundationalism in its own way as was Descartes's rationalist position. The expressivist theory of language had to be invented to account for moral language because of agreement on the assumption that *ordinarily* language works by referring and representing. The idealist metaphysics of the modern period (G. W. F. Hegel, F. H. Bradley) was a reaction against the predominant materialist, atomist, and reductionist assumptions of modern science.[3]

My more nuanced claim is that modern thought has been structured by *debates* over knowledge, language, and metaphysics, in which position and

---

2. Toulmin, *Cosmopolis*, 1-4.

3. This claim about metaphysics is oversimplified. I shall address this issue more adequately in Chapter 6.

counter-position share certain underlying assumptions about the nature of justification, meaning, and the relation between parts and wholes. It is the recent critique and displacement of these underlying assumptions that justifies the claim that modern thought is being supplanted by new, postmodern ways of thinking.[4]

Second, the term *postmodern* has lately become associated with Continental schools of thought such as deconstructionism, a literary theory *cum* philosophy, whose best-known proponent is the French literary critic Jacques Derrida. Deconstructionism and allied schools derive from the heritage of the nineteenth-century German philosopher Friedrich Nietzsche, as well as from the nineteenth-century Swiss linguist Ferdinand de Saussure. I have argued elsewhere that these self-proclaimed postmodernists actually share too many assumptions with their modern predecessors to count as truly postmodern.[5] Consequently, my survey of postmodern thought will turn in another direction. There have been radical changes within the Anglo-American philosophical tradition, beginning in the middle of the twentieth century, which only now are being recognized for the epochal changes that they are. It is this Anglo-American postmodernism, I claim, that will prove to be of interest for transcending the besetting problems of modern theology.[6]

If we want a handy date to mark the beginning of the end of the modern period, I suggest 1951. It was the date of publication of W. V. O. Quine's "Two Dogmas of Empiricism," a highly respected article calling into question two of the positions necessary for a foundationalist account of knowledge. That year also marked the death of Ludwig Wittgenstein, whose later repudiation of his early work is a treasure house of insights not only for postmodern philosophy of language, but also for ways of moving beyond modern foundationalism and reductionism. All of Wittgenstein's postmodern writings were published posthumously.

---

4. I am much indebted to my husband for this view. See Nancey Murphy and James Wm. McClendon, Jr., "Distinguishing Modern and Postmodern Theologies," *Modern Theology* 5, no. 3 (April 1989): 191-214.

5. See Nancey Murphy, "Textual Relativism, Philosophy of Language, and the baptist Vision," in *Theology without Foundations*, ed. Stanley Hauerwas, Nancey Murphy, and Mark Nation (Nashville: Abingdon Press, 1994), 245-70.

6. For a more detailed account, see Nancey Murphy, *Anglo-American Postmodernity: Philosophical Perspectives on Science, Religion, and Ethics* (Boulder, CO: Westview Press, forthcoming). Note that the designations "Continental" and "Anglo-American" are not strictly geographical labels. During the past century or so two distinct and distinctive philosophical traditions have developed, and these are the conventional terms used to identify them, despite the facts that the Vienna Circle has had its major influence in the Anglo-American tradition, that many American philosophers work in the Continental tradition, that there are a significant number of analytic philosophers in Germany, and so on.

EPISTEMOLOGICAL HOLISM

Chapter 1 described the predominant modern view of knowledge as foundationalist. Recall that this is a theory about the justification of knowledge that imagines a belief system to be like a building, which cannot stand without a solid foundation—a "bottom layer" of beliefs that cannot be called into question. The replacement position is called holism.

The first crack in the foundationalist doctrine came with philosopher of science Karl Popper's admission that even if science is like a building, the facts that support it do not constitute a solid foundation. In 1935 he wrote:

> The empirical basis of objective science has thus nothing 'absolute' about it. Science does not rest upon solid bedrock. The bold structure of its theories rises, as it were, above a swamp. It is like a building erected on piles. The piles are driven down from above into the swamp, but not down to any natural or 'given' base; and if we stop driving the piles deeper, it is not because we have reached firm ground. We simply stop when we are satisfied that the piles are firm enough to carry the structure, at least for the time being.[7]

If modern theories of knowledge have been shaped by a metaphor, the image of knowledge as a building, it is to be expected that a new picture should mark the beginning of a new era. Quine has provided a new image: knowledge as a web or net.

> The totality of our so-called knowledge or beliefs, from the most casual matters of geography and history to the profoundest laws of atomic physics or even of pure mathematics and logic, is a man-made fabric which impinges on experience only along the edges. Or, to change the figure, total science is like a field of force whose boundary conditions are experience. A conflict with experience at the periphery occasions re-adjustments in the interior of the field. Truth values have to be redistributed over some of our statements. Re-evaluation of some statements entails re-evaluation of others, because of their logical interconnections—the logical laws being in turn simply certain further statements of the system. . . . But the total field is so underdetermined by its boundary conditions, experience, that there is much latitude of choice as to what statements to re-evaluate in the light of any single contrary experience. No particular experiences are linked with any particular statements in the interior of the field,

---

7. Karl Popper, *The Logic of Scientific Discovery* (New York: Harper, 1965); translation by Popper et al. of *Logik der Forschung* (Vienna, 1935).

except indirectly through considerations of equilibrium affecting the field as a whole.[8]

In this chapter we first consider the problems with foundationalism that make Quine's holist theory more appealing. We shall see that there are complications, discovered during the three-hundred-year history of modern epistemology, that have required so many "epicycles" that it now seems better to many to abandon the foundationalist model and begin afresh with a new one. Along the way I shall mention some critiques of "inside-out" epistemology.

Next, we consider Quine's holist epistemology in somewhat more detail, attempting to understand how it does and does not differ from foundationalist theories. A few theologians, such as Ronald Thiemann, have already made use of Quine's work, and we shall have to see what a Quinian theological method looks like. The application of Quine's holism to theology, however, brings out a critical problem not apparent when the model was used only in the spheres of everyday knowledge and science—relativism. I shall claim that this is the besetting problem for the postmodern epistemological era.

Consequently, the next step in this chapter is to consider solutions proposed to the problem Quine's image conjures up—the worry that there are competing webs of equally consistent beliefs, and that there is no rational way to choose among them. Already, since the publication of Quine's article, there have been significant developments in this new approach to knowledge. In the philosophy of science we see an important line of development from Popper to Thomas Kuhn and Imre Lakatos.

I shall claim that the most useful development for theological purposes is the epistemological work of Alasdair MacIntyre. MacIntyre was stimulated by the aforementioned developments in philosophy of science, but also by his own work in moral philosophy and his quest for an understanding of practical reasoning that would avoid moral relativism.

Lakatos and MacIntyre have made such important amendments to Quinean and Kuhnian holism that their views deserve a name of their own. I shall label their theories *historicist-holism*.

Finally, we must enquire what difference the new historicist-holist epistemology will make to theology. Some speculation is in order here, since these resources are too recent to have received wide attention in theological circles. Of course, my hope is that this chapter will help change that fact. My prediction is that historicist-holism will provide much more useful resources for understanding theological method (and perhaps for reforming the theological craft) than did the foundationalist model. If this happens, I expect to see a softening of the distinctions between liberal and conservative theologians. In

---

8. W. V. O. Quine, "Two Dogmas of Empiricism," in *From a Logical Point of View* (Cambridge: Harvard University Press, 1953), 20-46; quotation 42-43. Originally published in 1951.

place of a dichotomy there should be a spectrum of theological approaches ranging from the postliberal theologies of the Yale school to something we as yet have no name for. We might call them postmodern evangelicals.[9]

PROBLEMS WITH FOUNDATIONALISM

Foundationalist philosophers have pursued two broad strategies in seeking categories of beliefs suited to serve as justification for the rest of knowledge. We can call these the empiricist and rationalist strategies. I shall try to show that there is a corollary of Murphy's Law working against the foundationalist epistemologist[10]: whenever one finds suitably indubitable beliefs to serve as a foundation, they will always turn out to be useless for justifying any interesting claims; beliefs that are useful for justifying other claims will always turn out not to be indubitable, and in fact will be found to be dependent upon the structure they are intended to justify.

The empiricist strategy is represented in the early modern period by Locke's knowledge based on "ideas" originating in sense perception, and by David Hume's "impressions." The logical positivists renewed the quest for empiricist foundations, picking up almost exactly where Hume had left the discussion a century and a half earlier.

Recall that the motivation for the modern empiricists' "inside-out" approach to knowledge was the recognition that ordinary reports about what one perceives are corrigible. To provide the requisite foundational certitude, it was necessary to retrench and make claims only about one's perceptions themselves. Thus, "ideas" or later "sense-data"—mental objects of perception— were called upon by philosophers to serve as the true foundation for empirical knowledge. Instead of claims such as "I see a brown dog," one could make the safer claim that "I seem to be seeing a brown dog," or "I am having a brown canoid appearance." I might be wrong about the dog, but it is difficult to imagine how I could be wrong about the appearance. Philosophers use the term *incorrigible* to refer to such claims, meaning that they are indubitable because there is no imaginable way they could be overridden or corrected.

However, the positivists quickly realized that the gain in certitude of the foundation was offset by new difficulties in construction: the problem of how to *use* these appearance-statements to justify claims about a real, objective world. Recognizing more loss than gain in the turn to sense-data,

---

9. Roger E. Olsen has suggested "postconservative evangelical." See "Postconservative Evangelicals Greet the Postmodern Age," in *The Christian Century* (May 1995): 480-83. However, *postconservative* is not a suitable description since conservatism (favoring the past in a contest between traditional formulations and contemporary relevance) will continue to characterize one end of the spectrum.

10. Murphy's Law in its simplest formulation states that "whatever can go wrong will."

some of the logical positivists and all of their successors (the neo-positivists) turned their attention to ordinary scientific facts. Among these latter philosophers of science was Karl Popper, quoted above. Popper and his fellows recognized both that the facts themselves could be called into question and that the structure of scientific theory resting on these "piles" was only probable.

What finally brought empiricist foundationalism to an end was the recognition that scientific facts are "theory-laden." N. R. Hanson argued that the kind of observations that support scientific theories are more like seeing that a battery is charged or seeing that a wound is septic than like seeing color patches. To describe an observation as, say, a crater, is already to have a theory about its cause.[11]

Thomas Kuhn and others have pointed out not only that scientific facts are generally dependent upon theoretical interpretation, but also that the construction of the experimental apparatus with which the observations are made will require theoretical knowledge. For example, consider the wealth of theory involved in construction of an electron microscope and interpretation of the images it produces.

For this reason, if we are to hold to the picture of knowledge as a building, we now have to imagine the foundation partially suspended from a top-floor balcony![12]

The quest for rationalist foundations is a somewhat more complex story. Descartes described his foundational beliefs as "clear and distinct ideas," by which he meant ideas that he was unable to doubt. Locke used similar sorts of foundations for purposes such as his argument for the existence of God, but he described these premises as being derived from "relations of ideas," or equivalently, from reflection on the activity of his mind.

Descartes's strategy has been rejected by most philosophers simply because, in the passage of time, it has turned out that what is indubitable in one intellectual context is all too questionable in another; for example, the premise in Descartes's argument for the existence of God: "There must be at least as much reality in the efficient and total cause as in the effect."[13] It is difficult in our day even to understand what this means, let alone to know that it must be true.

As in the case of empirical foundations, there is a tradeoff between utility for justifying important claims and indubitability. On the one hand, Descartes's highly questionable premise about causes and quantities of reality is not only useful but indispensable in his argument for the existence of God. On the

---

11. See N. R. Hanson, *Patterns of Discovery* (Cambridge: Cambridge University Press, 1958).

12. Many philosophers argue that this is the case even with our simplest reports of perception—we already have to know a great deal about the world to know what we are seeing. See especially Wilfrid Sellars, *Science, Perception and Reality* (New York: Humanities Press, 1963).

13. Descartes, *Meditations on First Philosophy*, Third Meditation.

other, the *cogito ergo sum* ("I think, therefore I exist") has the requisite foundational certitude, but without proof of God's existence and the guarantee this provides for the veracity of sense experience, there is no way to argue from Descartes's solipsistic inner life to the existence of an external world.

Immanuel Kant's attempt to stake out a sphere of "synthetic a priori knowledge" was an important episode in the rationalist program. This knowledge was supposed to be safe from empirical falsification because it was based on the unchanging structure of the mind rather than on variable empirical events. Kant's work helped to formalize the distinction between empirical knowledge and *some* other kind of knowledge not dependent upon experience, but there has been no consensus about how to define this other kind of knowledge. Some of Kant's successors concentrated on formal systems, such as systems of logic or mathematics. It is now recognized that while deductive consequences of such systems are necessarily true, they are not necessarily true *of* anything. That is, when the move is made to apply them to reality—for example, to use a system of geometry for navigation in space—the trustworthiness of the calculations is no more certain than the axioms or than the (questionable) applicability of the terms of the system to physical quantities.

Others of Kant's successors attempted to distinguish, within ordinary knowledge, between an element that was dependent upon the way the world is and an element that was dependent only on the meanings of words or on the concepts employed. It was hoped that certitude could be found by concentrating on sentences wherein the empirical element came to nothing. Thus, for a time, philosophy was understood as conceptual analysis—a procedure expected to produce a body of knowledge safe from empirical refutation because it was based merely on the investigation of relations among concepts. In looking more closely at Quine's holism below, we shall see that the existence of any such knowledge was one of the dogmas that he has called into question.

Before moving on, though, it is important to see that rationalist foundations, like their empirical counterparts, turn out to be "hanging from the balcony."

A contemporary philosopher of religion who makes great use of the conceivability test to certify the premises of his arguments is Richard Swinburne. I once heard him present a paper in which he stated that it was conceivable that he should change into a crocodile and still remain himself. I found that quite inconceivable.[14]

How can it be that our intuitions could be so opposed? The explanation seems to be that he and I presuppose different theories about the nature of the person. Swinburne is a dualist; he identifies himself with his immaterial soul. Thus, he can easily imagine waking up one morning and finding that

---

14. In fact, I was so fascinated by the suggestion that I have completely forgotten what claim he was intending to support and the title of the paper.

his soul, the seat of his consciousness, personality, emotions, has transmigrated into the body of a crocodile—possible, though surely inconvenient. I presuppose a holist conception of the person, a nonreductive physicalism according to which human mental and spiritual capacities arise out of the complex ordering of our physical selves in their social environment.[15] On this view, no neo-cortex, no capacity for philosophical thought, no Swinburne.

This brief survey of foundationalist strategies shows that early hopes for certain foundations to justify all knowledge claims have been frustrated; I claim they always will be because of the tradeoff between the certitude and the usability of the foundations. Some thinkers accept this state of affairs but remain "chastened" foundationalists, keeping the foundationalist language and metaphors but adding a long list of qualifications to the theory.

However, there is good reason for abandoning the foundationalist picture altogether. There is no way, using this model, to represent the fact that the "foundations" are partially supported from above, as in the case of theory-laden data in science or presupposition-laden intuitions in philosophical arguments. For this reason, if for no other, we need a new picture, a new model, that will more adequately represent what we now know to be the case about knowledge.[16]

The foundationalist quest among modern theologians shows striking parallels to those in science and philosophy. When conservative theologians were forced to admit that the biblical texts contained contradictions, a common move was to argue that only the original autographs were inerrant. This claim is incorrigible (since all of these are lost) but the incorrigibility comes at the cost of needing to ground theology on something inaccessible to contemporary theologians; the lost autographs are inerrant but useless. This parallels the empiricists' move to (inaccessible) sense-data in the observer's mind. And parallel to the recognition of the theory-ladenness of scientific data is the recognition of the theory-ladenness of biblical interpretations—the hermeneutic circle.

We have already seen the liberal quest for an experience more basic and less corrigible than ordinary religious experience. One problem here is that no consensus has emerged regarding what this inner experience *is*. Also, two kinds of construction problems emerge. One is Feuerbachian skepticism about the reality of God (parallel to Cartesian solipsism); the other is that there seems to be no limit to the plurality of theologies that can be legitimated on the basis of such private experience.

If theologians make a move parallel to that of the neo-positivists—to recognize ordinary but fallible experience as the foundation—then again there is a problem parallel to that of the theory-ladenness of scientific data. Religious

---

15. See pp. 149-51 below.

16. For a more detailed discussion (with pictures) see Nancey Murphy, *Reasoning and Rhetoric in Religion* (Valley Forge, PA: Trinity Press International, 1994), esp. chap. 12.

experiences tend to reflect the theologies of those who have them. Thus, Catholics have visions of Christ and of Mary; Protestants have experiences of repentance and reconciliation; Hindus have experiences of Krishna.[17]

Perhaps at this point theologians too ought to be looking for a new conception of how justification works.

QUINEAN HOLISM

Apart from the picture—knowledge as a web or net—Quine's holist theory of knowledge differs in several important respects from foundationalism. First, there *need* be no intrinsically indubitable (unrevisable) beliefs; nor are there any sharp distinctions among types of belief, only degrees of differences in how far a belief is from the experiential boundary.

Second, as I pointed out above, for foundationalists, reasoning (construction) goes in only one direction—up from the foundation. For holists, in contrast, there is no preferred direction of reasoning, and the kinds of connections among beliefs in the web are many: strict logical implication, weaker probabilistic arguments, arguments "forward" to further conclusions; arguments "backward" to presuppositions. This allows holists to take account of the fact, recognized above, that the data (scientific facts, interpretations of texts, or whatever) are theory-laden, partially dependent on theoretical knowledge.

In general, *holism* means that each belief is supported by its ties to its neighboring beliefs and, ultimately, to the whole. *Justification consists in showing that problematic beliefs are closely tied to beliefs that we have no good reason to call into question.* So the coherence of the web is crucial for justification. When inconsistencies appear—conflicts within the web or with "recalcitrant experience"—there are always a number of ways to revise in order to restore consistency. The choices that will be made here are in a sense pragmatic: how to mend the web with as little disturbance to the whole as possible. As a matter of practice, some beliefs, such as the laws of logic, are held immune from revision except under the most extreme pressure from the experiential boundary, since, with their central location, to change them would necessitate changes throughout the web.[18]

The two dogmas that Quine called into question in his 1951 article were, first, the belief that each justifiable belief could be traced to special (foundational) beliefs derived directly from experience. Rather, it is the whole of

---

17. Steven T. Katz, "Language, Epistemology, and Mysticism," in *Mysticism and Philosophical Analysis,* ed. Steven T. Katz (New York: Oxford University, 1978), 22-74.

18. An instance of empirical pressure on logic is seen in the claim that quantum uncertainty calls for a three-valued logic, in which statements can be true, false, or indeterminate.

our knowledge that faces the tribunal of experience. Second, the attempt to salvage a special indubitable kind of knowledge based on concepts and their relations fails because we are always able, and sometimes willing, to adjust the meanings of terms in order to maintain the truth of the claims. In other words, concepts themselves have a history, and their meaning shifts under the pressure of new discoveries and theoretical changes.

NONFOUNDATIONAL THEOLOGICAL METHOD

If, as I suggest, a holist theory is a more adequate model of how justification of knowledge claims works, there ought to be significant consequences for how theologians engage in and explain their task.

In the first half of the book, which dealt with modern theology, it was necessary to limit exposition to selected theological examples. However, theologians who have consciously adopted a nonfoundational approach are, so far, few enough that it would be possible to survey them all in a longer book. The easiest group to recognize here is the Yale school. This includes Hans Frei, Paul Holmer, David Kelsey, and George Lindbeck, professors or former professors at Yale, and some of their students, including Ronald Thiemann, William Werpehowski, William Placher, Charles Wood, and Kathryn Tanner. Some would include the theological ethicist Stanley Hauerwas here as well.

Others have come to their nonfoundational positions by other routes: James Wm. McClendon, Jr., through study of J. L. Austin's philosophy of language; John Howard Yoder (as far as I can tell) simply from reflection on the nature of biblical, ethical, and theological reasoning; the present author through familiarity with nonfoundational philosophy of science.

An important question that needs to be settled in order to give an account of the historical origins of nonfoundational theology (but one that will not be tackled here) is how to understand Karl Barth. Some see him as the first great anti-foundationalist theologian,[19] and as such a major influence on Lindbeck, Hauerwas, Yoder, and others. However, Barth is certainly open to being read as a scriptural foundationalist, even in passages quoted by those arguing against this claim! "God's revelation is a ground which has no higher or deeper ground above or below it but is an absolute ground in itself, and therefore for man a court from which there can be no possible appeal to a higher court."[20]

In this chapter we look at the contributions of two members of the Yale school: first, Thiemann and then, more briefly, Lindbeck. It is important to

---

19. John Thiel includes him in his survey in *Nonfoundationalism*, along with Lindbeck, Thiemann, Tanner, and Frei.

20. Karl Barth, quoted by Thiel, *Nonfoundationalism*, p. 50 (unfortunately without citing the location in *Church Dogmatics*).

note that while these two do fall into the category of nonfoundational or holist theology, they alone do not define the category. That is, there are special historical factors that have shaped their approaches to theology along with the influence of nonfoundational philosophers. One of these is the fact that their theological antecedents are largely of a liberal rather than conservative type—Lindbeck calls himself a "post-*liberal*" theologian. It remains to be seen what will develop when conservative theologians consciously adopt holist methodologies.

A second factor shaping the particular character of the theology of the Yale school is Frei's contribution. Frei's concerns focused on the history of biblical hermeneutics. In *The Eclipse of Biblical Narrative* he spoke to the question how it came about that for centuries the biblical narratives were read realistically, that is, assuming that in the first instance they are *about* what they first seem to be about. Yet in modern hermeneutics and theology (he should say, modern theology of the liberal type) they have been taken to be about something else—in biblical studies, in light of historical-critical methods, about the (very different) history *behind* the text; in theology, about the religious self-awareness of Jesus and his disciples, or existential orientation, or whatever.

Simply pointing to this exceedingly significant change in how the texts are now read led Frei's colleagues to attempt a *recovery* of the traditional reading strategies. This attempt has turned out to be compatible with the change from foundational to nonfoundational epistemology. One point of contact with nonfoundationalism is Frei's diagnosis of the modern turn as being due to a quest for foundations more secure than the text itself.

Ronald Thiemann follows Frei in his interest in the narrative shape of much of the Bible.[21] His book is fascinating, from the point of view of the present study, because his concern is not only with developing and using a nonfoundationalist (holist) theological method, but also with showing how modern theories of knowledge have distorted the Christian doctrine of revelation in trying to make Scripture serve as an epistemological foundation. He provides three case studies (Locke, Schleiermacher, and Thomas Torrance) showing that these motives have produced "discussions of revelation [that] have created complex conceptual and epistemological tangles that are difficult to understand and nearly impossible to unravel" (1). As a consequence, some have argued that the very concept of revelation is unintelligible.

Thiemann's goal is to disentangle the concept of revelation from its modern epistemological duties and explicate it, instead, in traditional terms of God's *prevenience*:

> Christian theology has traditionally been guided by the conviction that faith's knowledge of God is a gift bestowed through God's free grace.

---

21. See Ronald F. Thiemann, *Revelation and Theology: The Gospel as Narrated Promise* (Notre Dame: University of Notre Dame Press, 1985).

Our thought and speech about God are not simply the free creations of human imagination but are developed in obedient response to God's prior initiative. Theologians have commonly referred to this prior act of God as revelation (2).

In order to accomplish his goal, Thiemann first gives an account of holist justification of a theological claim, then uses that method to show the warranted assertability of the doctrine of God's prevenience.

Borrowing directly from Quine,[22] Thiemann states that holist justification consists in seeking the relation between a disputed belief and the web of interrelated beliefs within which it rests.

Holism understands justification as a process of rational persuasion. "We convince someone of something by appealing to beliefs he already holds and by combining these to induce further beliefs in him, step by step, until the belief we wanted finally to inculcate in him is inculcated."[23]

Thiemann claims that belief in God's prevenience is logically tied both to beliefs and to practices that are not in dispute among Christians and, further, that these beliefs and practices are so central to Christian identity that to give them up would constitute a drastic change in Christian identity. The *direction* of Thiemann's reasoning is "backward" from these beliefs and practices to prevenience as a presupposition upon which they depend.

One of the Christian practices that depends for its intelligibility on the doctrine of divine prevenience is the eucharist, a word that means literally "thanksgiving." If God has not acted graciously in the past, then what is there to give thanks *for*? The whole of Scripture can be read as a complex identity narrative, telling who God is by recounting his deeds—his promises and fulfillment of those promises in history. Praise, supplication, thanksgiving, all become meaningless without the presupposition of God's prior reality and action.[24]

While deeply indebted to Quine, Thiemann's account of theological method is actually more sophisticated in several ways than Quine's epistemology. First, he recognizes the intrinsic relationship between human knowing and doing. It is not merely consistency among beliefs that rationality requires, but also consistency between belief and action. This theme will be pursued in Chapter 5.

---

22. Especially from W. V. O. Quine and J. S. Ullian, *The Web of Belief* (New York: Random House, 1970).

23. Thiemann, *Revelation and Theology*, 75-76; quoting from Quine and Ullian, *The Web of Belief*, 127.

24. Note again the deep connections between conceptions of divine action and theories of knowledge (revelation) and language.

Second, Thiemann recognizes a historical dimension in the justification of beliefs. That is, webs of belief endure and change through time, and part of what consistency requires is congruity with past formulation. This does not mean slavish repetition of the past, but enough continuity so we can say that this version of, say, the doctrine of prevenience is a reformulation of the same doctrine as taught by Augustine and Luther. This is a more sophisticated version of Quine's recognition of the value of conservatism in matters epistemological.

Finally, Quine counts the laws of logic as part of the web of belief. This claim needs to be extended to recognize that all sorts of standards of rationality are internal to traditions. Thiemann recognizes this, claiming that part of the theologian's description of the "internal logic of the Christian faith" is recognition and employment of "criteria of judgment internal to the Christian tradition" (74). More on this tradition-constituted character of rationality below.

PROBLEMS WITH HOLISM

The foundationalist picture of knowledge induced its own peculiar epistemological worries: what if there is no foundation? Or, more ridiculous still: what if the foundation appears to be hanging from the balcony? Quine's picture of knowledge as a web relieves the foundationalist's worry—there is no "place" in the web for a foundation, so its absence does not lead to skepticism. The logical "threads" in a web necessarily run in both directions—the nodes are mutually supportive—so the theory-dependence of data is a virtue rather than a vice.

However, this same picture induces its own special epistemological worry. We can imagine, alongside our own web, a variety of competing webs, and the question then arises how to choose among them.

This worry may have already crossed the reader's mind in considering Thiemann's account of theology. In order to justify the problematic claim for God's prevenience, Thiemann had to presuppose a great deal of the rest of Christian belief and practice. He states explicitly that nonfoundational theology is located squarely within the Christian community and tradition and seeks to redescribe the *internal* logic of the Christian faith. He contrasts this approach to that of trying to defend Christian truth-claims in light of general principles of rationality. One may well ask, then, are the beliefs *and epistemological standards* of a convictional community simply up to them?

Quine is apparently not bothered by relativist worries. He takes the web of beliefs to comprise the whole of knowledge. It is possible gradually to alter the whole, but it is impossible to imagine replacing the whole thing at once—this would not be epistemological revolution but madness. There is an engaging image used by a variety of philosophers comparing knowledge to a ship at sea: we can repair it plank by plank, but we can never rebuild it all at once from the bottom up.

But Quine has a fairly circumscribed view of what counts as knowledge: science, logic, and everyday knowledge of the sensible world. It may well be unthinkable that there could be radically different versions of this network; however, not only theologians but social scientists, anthropologists, and others are aware of a proliferation of competing theologies, religions, worldviews. So if Quine is not worried about relativism, perhaps he should be.

Whether he intended to or not, Thomas Kuhn has provided powerful arguments for relativism in philosophy of science. Kuhn provided a thoroughly holist account of scientific knowledge. Science progresses by means of the development of paradigms.[25] Paradigms are complex systems incorporating facts, theories, metaphysical assumptions, and research ideals that arise from emulating the scientific work recorded in a particularly influential text, such as Newton's *Principia* or Lavoisier's *Chemistry*. Progress in science is discontinuous; periods of problem-solving within a paradigm are interrupted by revolutionary phases when the paradigm falls into crisis and is replaced by a new one. The holist features of this account of science are, first, that paradigms are evaluated and replaced as a whole; and second, that the theoretical elements of the paradigm help determine what will count as facts—the thesis of the theory-ladenness of data.

So the language in philosophy of science is a bit different from Quine's and the unit of analysis is different (paradigms versus total webs of belief), but most of the worrisome claims are the same: Data are theory-laden and hence underdetermined by experience. Theory is underdetermined by data. Radically different theories are supported by different domains of data, or at least by differently interpreted data.

In addition, we have in Kuhn's survey of paradigm changes compelling evidence of radical conceptual changes in science; there is also the claim that the scientific worldviews employing these different concepts are incommensurable—not translatable one to another. However, the most significant contribution Kuhn makes to the relativist's resources is his claim that standards of rationality are paradigm dependent. This is a less radical position than Quine's claim that logical "beliefs" are themselves but a part of the web and thus subject to revision in light of experience. But Kuhn's claim that at least some standards for evaluation of paradigms are historically conditioned has been more widely accepted and has thus had a greater impact on epistemology.

So justification of belief now involves two sorts of questions: Is this particular belief justifiable within the particular web to which it belongs?—and here we know how to proceed. Is this web of beliefs (or paradigm, or theo-

---

25. Thomas Kuhn, *The Structure of Scientific Revolutions*, 2d ed. (Chicago: University of Chicago Press, 1970).

logical system) justified (or justifiable) over against its competitors?—and here it is not yet clear how we are to proceed.

This difficulty appears in Lindbeck's discussion of truth. Lindbeck devises three concepts of truth. First, intrasystematic truth is truth of coherence. "Utterances are intrasystematically true when they cohere with the total relevant context,"[26] which involves first-order religious language (prayer, preaching, and so on) and the practices of the community. Theology is second-order discourse and it must cohere with both first-order language and with practice.

A second sort of truth is categorial truth:

> The questions raised in comparing religions have to do first of all with the adequacy of their categories. Adequate categories are those which can be made to apply to what is taken to be real, and which therefore make possible, though they do not guarantee, propositional, practical, and symbolic truth. A religion that is thought of as having such categories can be said to be "categorially true" (48).

Finally, there is ontological truth, or truth of correspondence. But Lindbeck's definition is quite different from what one might expect. A religion is ontologically true if it constitutes "a form of life, a way of being in the world, which itself corresponds to the Most Important, the Ultimately Real" (65).

So intrasystematic truth correlates with the epistemological question of how we justify a particular statement, given the rest of the web. The interesting twist is the role of practices here. Categorial truth and ontological truth correlate with the epistemological question of how we justify this entire web of beliefs (and practices) over against its competitors. Lindbeck has no answer here, so we must look to epistemological theories more advanced than Quine's and Lindbeck's, with their emphasis on coherence.[27]

HISTORICIST-HOLISM: IMRE LAKATOS

Imre Lakatos, another holist philosopher of science, took up the challenge implicit in Kuhn's work: how to judge rationally between competing paradigms (or "research programs," as Lakatos preferred to call them), despite

---

26. Lindbeck, *The Nature of Doctrine*, 64.

27. I have suggested that Lindbeck's conception of truth is likely to be unsatisfactory for postmodern evangelicals and that Alasdair MacIntyre has made a more promising proposal in *Whose Justice? Which Rationality?* (Notre Dame: University of Notre Dame Press, 1988), chap. 18. See Nancey Murphy, "Philosophical Resources for Postmodern Evangelical Theology," in *Christian Scholars Review* (forthcoming).

the facts that there are no theory-independent data and that standards for good scientific research are paradigm-dependent. His central insight is that research programs can be compared on the basis of *how they change over time* in response to problematic empirical discoveries.

Lakatos described a research program as follows: There is a network of theoretical assertions supported by a body of data. One theory, the "hard core," is central to the research program. Conjoined to the core are a set of auxiliary hypotheses that together add enough information to allow the data to be related to the theory. Examples of types of auxiliary hypotheses are theories of observation or of instrumentation, lower-level theories that apply the core theory in different kinds of cases, and so forth. The auxiliary hypotheses form a "protective belt" around the hard core, since they can be modified when potentially falsifying data are found. A research program, then, is a temporally extended series of complex theories whose core remains the same while auxiliary hypotheses are successively modified, replaced, or amplified in order to account for problematic observations.

The problem in evaluating research programs is that, given enough ingenuity on the part of the scientists, any conflicting datum (anomaly) can be made consistent with the program by adding theoretical explanations. To illustrate his point, Lakatos tells the following story of an imaginary challenge to Newtonian dynamics:

> The story is about an imaginary case of planetary misbehavior. A physicist of the pre-Einstein era takes Newton's mechanics and his law of gravitation, (N), the accepted initial conditions, I, and calculates, with their help, the path of a newly discovered small planet, p. But the planet deviates from the calculated path. Does our Newtonian physicist consider that the deviation was forbidden by Newton's theory and therefore that, once established, it refutes the theory N? No. He suggests that there must be a hitherto unknown planet p′ which perturbs the path of p. He calculates the mass, orbit, etc., of this hypothetical planet and then asks an experimental astronomer to test his hypothesis. The planet p′ is so small that even the biggest available telescopes cannot possibly observe it: the experimental astronomer applies for a research grant to build yet a bigger one. In three years' time the new telescope is ready. Were the unknown planet p′ to be discovered, it would be hailed as a new victory of Newtonian science. But it is not. Does our scientist abandon Newton's theory and his idea of the perturbing planet? No. He suggests that a cloud of cosmic dust hides the planet from us. He calculates the location and properties of this cloud and asks for a research grant to send up a satellite to test his calculations. Were the satellite's instruments (possibly new ones, based on a little-tested theory) to record the existence of the conjectural cloud, the result would be hailed as an outstanding victory for Newtonian science. But the cloud is not found. Does our scientist abandon Newton's

theory, together with the idea of the perturbing planet and the idea of the cloud which hides it? No. He suggests that . . . [28]

In reading this account, one wonders whether Lakatos had read Antony Flew's parable of the Gardener:

> Once upon a time two explorers came upon a clearing in the jungle. In the clearing were growing many flowers and many weeds. One explorer says, "Some gardener must tend this plot." The other disagrees, "There is no gardener." So they pitch their tents and set a watch. No gardener is ever seen. "But perhaps he is an invisible gardener." So they set up a barbed-wire fence. They electrify it. They patrol with bloodhounds. (For they remember how H. G. Wells's *The Invisible Man* could be both smelt and touched though he could not be seen.) But no shrieks ever suggest that some intruder has received a shock. No movements of the wire ever betray an invisible climber. The bloodhounds never give cry. Yet still the Believer is not convinced. "But there is a gardener, invisible, intangible, insensible to electric shocks, a gardener who has no scent and makes no sound, a gardener who comes secretly to look after the garden which he loves." At last the Sceptic despairs, "But what remains of your original assertion? Just how does what you call an invisible, intangible, eternally elusive gardener differ from an imaginary gardener or even from no gardener at all?"[29]

These little stories suggest that both scientists and theologians have an interest in distinguishing between what Lakatos calls progressive and degenerating research programs. A degenerating research program is one whose core theory is saved by ad hoc modifications of the protective belt—mere face-saving devices, or linguistic tricks, as Lakatos called them. We have some sense of what these expressions mean, but it is difficult to propose criteria by which to rule out such nonscientific maneuvers. The heart of Lakatos's methodology is his characterization of the kinds of maneuvers that *are* scientifically acceptable. A research program is said to be *progressive* when new versions of the program not only account for the anomalies that provoked the changes but are also supported by novel, hitherto unexpected facts. In the stories above, if the existence of the dust cloud had been independently corroborated, the astronomical program would have been

---

28. Imre Lakatos, "Falsification and the Methodology of Scientific Research Programmes," in *The Methodology of Scientific Research Programmes: Philosophical Papers Volume I,* ed. John Worrall and Gregory Currie (Cambridge: Cambridge University Press, 1978), 8-101; quotation, 16-17.

29. Antony Flew, "Theology and Falsification," in *New Essays in Philosophical Theology,* ed. Antony Flew and Alasdair MacIntyre (London: SCM Press, 1955), 96-99; quotation, 96.

shown to be progressive. If the bloodhounds had detected an intruder, this confirmation of the existence of invisible men would have been novel indeed!

I have argued elsewhere that Lakatos's methodology can be used in theology, since theologians are tempted to the same sort of ad hoc theorizing as are scientists. Here the facts would be results of biblical studies, historical data, and the sorts of religious experience that are open to communal discernment and communal agreement. Doctrines play the role of theories. The hard core would be some "single, synoptic, imaginative judgment" concerning "what Christianity is basically all about"[30]; for example, existential attitude (Bultmann), or expressions of religious awareness (Schleiermacher), or social ethics (John Howard Yoder). These competing theological programs can be compared on the basis of their relative progress or degeneration.[31] It is interesting that *scholasticism* has been adopted as a term for systems of thought that Lakatos would describe as degenerating—evidence of recognition on the part of theologians that such judgments could be made in theology.

However, many find the application of Lakatos's scientific terminology to theology jarring, and so it is welcome to find in the writings of Alasdair MacIntyre not only some important developments in historicist-holist epistemology but also a language for talking about knowledge and justification with which theologians are likely to feel more at home.

ALASDAIR MACINTYRE AND THEOLOGICAL METHOD

MacIntyre has had wide-ranging philosophical interests over the course of his career. Recently he has been best known as a philosophical ethicist. He reached his mature positions on epistemological issues through considering the question, what would it take to justify *a tradition of moral enquiry?*[32] Despite the difference in content (ethics versus science) it is clear that MacIntyre's insights parallel those of Lakatos.

According to MacIntyre, a tradition always begins with some contingent historical starting point—an authority of some sort, usually a text or set of texts. A tradition is a historically extended, socially embodied argument about how best to interpret and apply the formative text(s). All traditions

---

30. Cf. David Kelsey, *The Uses of Scripture in Recent Theology* (Philadelphia: Fortress, 1975), 159.

31. See Nancey Murphy, *Theology in the Age of Scientific Reasoning* (Ithaca, NY: Cornell University Press, 1990).

32. MacIntyre raised the question of the justification of a moral tradition in *After Virtue*, especially in the postscript added to the second edition (Notre Dame: University of Notre Dame Press, 1984). *Whose Justice? Which Rationality?* (Notre Dame: University of Notre Dame Press, 1988); and idem, *Three Rival Versions of Moral Enquiry: Encyclopaedia, Genealogy, and Tradition* (Notre Dame: University of Notre Dame Press, 1989) are devoted to this topic.

tend to go through similar stages. In the first stage the authorities have not yet been called into question. In the second stage inadequacies are identified—inconsistencies, resourcelessness in the face of theoretical or practical problems, challenges from other traditions. In a third stage the tradition is reformulated and elaborated in order to meet these inadequacies. The new version is obviously justified over its predecessor because it solves the problem its predecessor could not solve. This aspect of MacIntyre's theory is quite similar to Lakatos's concept of a progressive research program.[33]

It is important to note something that MacIntyre never says about traditions, but rather shows in his historical accounts: traditions can be contained within other traditions. Among the cases he has discussed, the Thomist tradition is part of the Augustinian tradition, which in turn is part of the Christian tradition. But the containment relation is not a simple one like a set of Russian dolls. Thomas and his followers also constitute a sub-tradition within the moral tradition that takes the concept of virtue as its starting point and traces its origin to the Homeric epics. So the applicability of MacIntyre's concept to theology does not depend on our being able to devise a single account of how the Christian tradition divides into sub-traditions. There will be many ways to cut up intellectual history, depending on our interests: we may divide theologians into modern conservative and liberal traditions as I have done here, but for other purposes denominational differences will be more important.

Let us see what features MacIntyre's account brings out if we think of Christian theologians as participating in the development of the Christian tradition. His work has important implications for the topic of the authority of Scripture. David Kelsey has written that the statement "Christian scripture is authoritative for Christian theology" is analytic.[34] This is a nonfoundational treatment of Scripture; there is no need for Christian theologians to justify taking the Scriptures as authoritative for theology, since to do so is what it *means* to be a Christian theologian. Notice, also, that this claim can now be seen as but a special case of MacIntyre's claim that *all* traditions are constituted by their acceptance of some authority. This is as true in science, according to Kuhn, as it is in theology. Thus, Christians need no special pleading to take Christian Scripture as authoritative. Of course this simply pushes the apologetic question back a step: how, now, to adjudicate among competing traditions, each with its own authoritative texts? We take up this issue in the next section.

I defined a tradition as an argument about how best to *interpret* and apply the formative texts. While MacIntyre does not say this (as far as I know), we may note that scriptural interpretation fits his (technical) definition of a *practice*:

---

33. See Alasdair MacIntyre, "Epistemological Crises, Dramatic Narrative, and the Philosophy of Science," *Monist* 60 (1977): 453-72; reprinted in *Paradigms and Revolutions*, ed. Gary Gutting (Notre Dame: University of Notre Dame Press, 1981).

34. Kelsey, *The Uses of Scripture in Recent Theology*, 99.

By a 'practice' I am going to mean any coherent and complex form of socially established cooperative human activity through which goods internal to that form of activity are realized in the course of trying to achieve those standards of excellence which are appropriate to, and partially definitive of, that form of activity, with the result that human powers to achieve excellence, and human conceptions of the ends and goods involved, are systematically extended.[35]

Practices develop in part through arguments intended to clarify and extend the conception of the goods at which the practices aim. Note how well this account describes the development of Christians' understanding of the *practice* of scriptural interpretation. As many of the arguments in biblical studies are over the proper *aims* of biblical criticism as over particular findings. And the conclusions of these arguments will have consequences concerning what aspects of the texts are important for theological purposes.

There are points of contact between MacIntyre's account of tradition-constituted rationality and recent developments in understanding biblical interpretation promoted by the Yale school, many of which reflect the appropriation of postmodern philosophy of language (described in the next chapter). One is recognition of the role of the community in interpretation—both MacIntyre and these recent theologians recognize that understanding is bound up with communal practices. Also, these contemporary biblical scholars and theologians reject the attempt to bring the Bible into the modern world and argue that contemporary interpreters must instead attempt to enter the world of the Bible. This conception of interpretation parallels MacIntyre's account of traditions as essentially socially embodied applications of formative texts—we *live* in our traditions and can only think and perceive by means of the categories, images, stories they provide.

If the above definition of a tradition guarantees an authoritative role for Scripture, it also guarantees a role for experience. The emphasis on social embodiment and application of the texts is another consequence of the Anglo-American postmodern recognition that language and knowledge are not over against the world, and therefore needing to be compared or related to it, but rather that language and knowledge are part of the social world. That there can be no theology that does not in one way or another take account of contemporary experience follows from this emphasis on social embodiment. The process of *applying* a text requires knowledge of the situation *to which* it is applied; application is necessarily (in the sense of logical necessity) a product of that which is applied and that to which it is applied. And this application will not be an ivory-tower exercise if a tradition is by definition socially embodied.

Consequently, experience is just as necessary a contributor to theology as the formative texts, and the opposition between Scripture and experience as

---

35. MacIntyre, *After Virtue*, 187.

sources of theology dissolves. But note how different a sense of experience this is from the modern liberals' inner awareness. Among the many definitions of *experience*, the most apt here is "active participation in events or activities, leading to the accumulation of knowledge or skill," and also "the totality of such events in the past of an individual or group."[36]

So, to revert to some Quinean terminology, the theologian can be imagined to be contributing to the reweaving of the doctrinal web as it has been handed on to her, whether this means minor repairs or a radical reformulation to meet an epistemological crisis in her tradition. In this reweaving she will be responsible to the formative texts, understood in light of the long development of communal practices of interpretation, but also responsible to that to which the texts are applied—the boundary conditions provided by current experience, in the broad sense described above: the life of the church in the world. Past experience of the community will necessarily have played a role in shaping earlier doctrinal formulations, and, depending on her community's attitude toward tradition (in the ordinary non-MacIntyrean sense), in her reweaving she may or may not be responsible to earlier formulations such as creeds or writings of reformers.

I believe much more of value could be found in MacIntyre's description of the development of traditions for describing the theologian's craft. However, the pressing question for all holist epistemologies, as I noted above, is that of relativism.

AGAINST RELATIVISM

In MacIntyre's Gifford Lectures, titled *Three Rival Versions of Moral Enquiry*, he says that his purpose is to show that it is *not* the case that rational debate between members of widely different systems of thought is impossible and to show, furthermore, that one party *can* emerge as undoubtedly rationally superior. The short answer as to how this is possible is that one of the standpoints may fail on its own terms (5). The relativistic worries associated with holist epistemology arise from recognition that standards of rationality do not stand outside the history of traditions, but rather develop within them:

> A tradition will move through stages, at each of which a justification of the scheme of beliefs as a whole could be supplied in terms of its rational superiority to the formulations of its predecessor, and that predecessor in turn justified by a further reference backward. But the availability of this type of reference from the present to the past is not by itself sufficient to constitute a tradition of rational enquiry. It is necessary also that a certain continuity of directedness emerge, so that

---

36. *The American Heritage Dictionary*, 2d college ed. (Boston: Houghton Mifflin Co., 1985).

theoretical and practical goals to guide enquiry are formulated and at later stages reformulated. Notice that among the beliefs and belief-presupposing practices which are subject to reformulation as a rationally mature tradition moves through its various stages may be, and characteristically are, both those which concern what it is to evaluate beliefs and practices as more or less rational, what truth is and how rationality and truth are connected, and those which concern the theoretical and practical goals toward which at each stage those participating in that particular tradition are directing themselves (116).

This tradition-dependence of standards for evaluation of beliefs and practices gives rise to the suspicion that, from within, every tradition will always appear to be justified on the basis of its own standards. MacIntyre's answer is to show that *this is simply not the case.* A tradition fails on its own terms when a solution to an epistemological crisis cannot be found (a reformulation of the tradition in continuity with earlier interpretations of its formative texts) that measures up to the tradition's own internal standards of rationality.

MacIntyre confirms that such failure is possible by recounting the history of the failure of the Thomist tradition's early rivals; he then argues for the superiority of his contemporary version of Thomism over its two most significant current rivals. It is not possible to summarize all of this here, so we look at only one example. MacIntyre argues that Thomas's ability to incorporate Aristotle into the Augustinian tradition showed his system to be clearly superior to those of the rival Augustinians. Catholics tend to take it for granted that this synthesis *counted* as success, but we need justification for this claim. Such justification can only be based on the epistemological standards of the Augustinian tradition itself.

The Augustinian tradition involved a modified Platonic epistemology in which God was conceived as light to the mind. The intellect is directed by a fallen will; thus, the will needs a kind of redirection toward the true and the good that will enable it to trust a teacher. Faith in authority has to precede rational understanding.

> By accepting authority . . . one acquires a teacher who both introduces one to certain texts and educates one into becoming the sort of person capable of reading those texts with understanding, texts in which such a person discovers the story of him or herself, including the story of how he or she was transformed into a reader of these texts. This story of oneself is embedded in the history of the world, an overall narrative within which all other narratives find their place.[37]

Thus, the Augustinian is committed to belief that no substantive rationality, independent of faith, will be able to provide an adequate vindication of

---

37. MacIntyre, *Three Rival Versions of Moral Enquiry,* 92.

its claims. All others will exhibit their own failures by falling into incoherence or acknowledgment of positions that cannot be justified. Augustinianism requires not only progress in solution of its own problems but also further confirmation by the way rival projects of intellectual and practical enquiry exhibit incoherence or resourcelessness. Correspondingly, it is put in question by the success of such rival projects (101-2).

The challenge to Augustinianism in Thomas's day from the newly rediscovered Aristotelian system was extreme: not only a rival account of what science is, but one that did not require divine illumination. For Aristotelians, the mind's potential adequacy to all its objects is a central tenet. There were also differences between the two philosophies in their very conceptions of truth, in accounts of the source of error, and in concepts of imagination and perception.

So Augustinian theologians at the University of Paris were faced with a crisis:

> Admit the Aristotelian corpus into the scheme of studies and you thereby confront the student with not one, but two claims upon his allegiance, claims which at key points are mutually exclusive. Exclude the Aristotelian corpus from the scheme of studies and you put in question both the universal, integrative claims of Augustinianism and the claims of the university, at least as understood at Paris. It was on the ability of the protagonists of Augustinianism to resolve the issues posed by this dilemma that the fate of their doctrine turned, something which became increasingly more evident in each successive decade of the thirteenth century (103).

This is the background against which Thomas's success at incorporating Aristotelian philosophy into Augustinian theology is to be appreciated.

So MacIntyre is arguing not that the ability to incorporate rival traditions is a universal standard for judging traditions, but rather that the Augustinian tradition's own account of the nature of knowledge, with its claims regarding its own universality and the fallibility of reason unaided by faith, made the incorporation imperative. Augustinianism would have *failed on its own terms* had this not been possible. MacIntyre has comparable arguments concerning the failure of the Aristotelian tradition on its own terms. Thus, he claims that Thomas's synthesis was clearly rationally superior to both of its major rivals, Augustinianism alone and the Aristotelian tradition alone, according to the only viable standards of rationality available at the time. Of course history has marched ahead, and new rivals with their own accounts of rationality have to be dealt with.[38]

---

38. For a more detailed assessment of MacIntyre's answer to relativism, see Nancey Murphy, "Postmodern Non-relativism: Imre Lakatos, Theo Meyering, and Alasdair MacIntyre," *Philosophical Forum* 27, no. 1 (Fall 1995): 37-53; and idem, *Anglo-American Postmodernity*, chap. 3.

CONCLUSION

What we can say so far about nonfoundational, historicist-holist theological method is the following: Contributions to the Christian theological tradition must, by definition, take the Christian Scriptures as authoritative, but in its application of those texts, it must pay attention to the contemporary context. While the texts themselves are simply given, their interpretation will be affected by a variety of assumptions, including theological positions. So there is a degree of circularity—of nonlinear reasoning—in the internal justification of the tradition, as theologians, biblical scholars, and others seek coherence among doctrinal claims, textual interpretations, and interpretations of the history of that very tradition.

This broad overview does not prescribe particular methodological moves in biblical criticism or theological reasoning; these develop within particular Christian sub-traditions and are judged along with the sub-tradition itself. So the pressing epistemological question is whether and how these all-inclusive packages of concepts, doctrines, critical methods, and textual interpretations can be judged.

MacIntyre has provided solid historical evidence that such judgments are possible, as well as general guidance for making them in the future: a tradition is justified insofar as it can be shown to make progress on its own terms (overcome its own epistemological crises) while its live competitors fail (on their own terms) to do so. MacIntyre's claim is not that such judgments are easy, or that they can always be made; his concern is to rebut the relativist argument that all traditions will always appear to be justified "from inside."

The sort of historically conditioned judgments that MacIntyre's arguments provide will not satisfy theologians who are used to absolute claims, but I hope to have shown earlier in the chapter that such claims rested on false pretenses. In contrast to the rationalism that has dominated modernity, we see here a sort of reasonableness that is modest about its own powers.[39]

Perhaps the most interesting aspect of this development is that epistemology has lost the priority over other disciplines that it claimed in the modern period. If MacIntyre is right, theories of knowledge are dependent upon theories of human nature, and in many cases these anthropological theories are ultimately theological. Theology is needed to justify epistemology just as much as epistemology is needed to justify theological claims. To return to the metaphor with which we began this chapter: Stout's king has not come along to get theology's plays started again, but perhaps the queen is back in her rightful place.

---

39. Cf. Toulmin, *Cosmopolis*, 198-201.

5

Linguistic Holism
and Religious Language

INTRODUCTION

In Chapter 2 I included a quotation from Augustine's *Confessions* that Ludwig Wittgenstein used to convey the representational or referential theory of language—the theory that the meaning of language comes from the objects to which it refers. Here is the quotation again:

> When they (my elders) named some object, and accordingly moved towards something, I saw this and I grasped that the thing was called by the sound they uttered when they meant to point it out. . . . Thus, as I heard words repeatedly used in their proper places in various sentences, I gradually learnt to understand what objects they signified; and after I had trained my mouth to form these signs, I used them to express my own desires. (*Confessions*, I, 8.)

In *Philosophical Investigations* Wittgenstein comments on Augustine's statement and the theory it represents as follows:

> Augustine, we might say, does describe a system of communication; only not everything that we call language is this system. And one has to say this in many cases where the question arises "Is this an appropriate description or not?" The answer is: "Yes, it is appropriate, but only for this narrowly circumscribed region, not for the whole of what you were claiming to describe."
>
> It is as if someone were to say: "A game consists in moving objects about on a surface according to certain rules . . ." —and we replied: You seem to be thinking of board games, but there are others. You can

make your definition correct by expressly restricting it to those games (§3).

In this chapter we consider Wittgensteinian arguments for the inadequacy of both the referential and expressivist theories of language. Then we examine the revolutionary accounts of language developed in the middle of the twentieth century by Wittgenstein (1889-1951) and J. L. Austin (1911-1960). There are significant differences between the views of these two philosophers, yet they will provide complementary insights for a more adequate account of religious language.

We saw in the preceding chapter that a break with foundationalist theories of knowledge required the replacement of the metaphor of knowledge as a building with a new image—knowledge as a web or net. The revolutionary character of Austin's and Wittgenstein's work also involves a changed image. The modern (and ancient) metaphor has been language as a mirror or picture of reality. The new image is language as a tool or language as action. Both Austin and Wittgenstein emphasize the *use* of language to do things in the social world. We shall pay special attention to Austin's "speech-act theory."

I have described the work of Austin and Wittgenstein as revolutionary, and count it as a part of the development of Anglo-American postmodern thought, but this is a controversial claim. While the revolution in epistemology recounted in Chapter 4 is widely (although not universally) recognized, this linguistic "revolution" is not. Austin and Wittgenstein have a few followers among professional philosophers of language[1]; however, most prominent philosophers of language are pursuing projects that this book would count as modern, while the significant uses of Austin's and Wittgenstein's works are primarily in other disciplines. Thus, we might say that a revolution in philosophy of language was narrowly averted.

One of the areas in which these two philosophers have had a significant impact is in the philosophy of religion. We shall examine here the use made of Austin's speech-act theory by James Wm. McClendon, Jr., and James M. Smith.[2]

Next we take up the issue of biblical criticism. I shall argue that Austin's theory of language is useful for understanding scriptural interpretation. If we consider scriptural passages to be analogous to speech acts, we need to ask what each text is *doing*. From this point of view we see that each of

---

1. John Searle at the University of California at Berkeley is Austin's most noted disciple, although he has developed this approach in a direction that Austin would not approve. See *Speech Acts: An Essay in the Philosophy of Language* (London: Cambridge University Press, 1969).

2. In James Wm. McClendon, Jr., and James M. Smith, *Convictions: Defusing Religious Relativism* (Valley Forge, PA: Trinity Press International, 1994); revision of *Understanding Religious Convictions* (Notre Dame: University of Notre Dame Press, 1975).

several earlier approaches to biblical interpretation is a necessary component for answering the question, but none alone can be adequate.

Wittgenstein has had a significant influence on the Yale school, largely through the work of philosopher of religion Paul Holmer. We shall examine George Lindbeck's cultural-linguistic theory of religion, noting influences of both Wittgenstein and Austin.

Finally, I shall return to Donald Bloesch's account of biblical language and show that the points he is trying to make about the *propositional content* of *mythic language*, which to moderns may sound awkward if not oxymoronic, can be made easily and clearly using Austin's terminology. The conclusion of this chapter will be that while both representation and expression are essential *dimensions* of religious language, no theory that focuses on either alone will provide an adequate account of religious language.

WITTGENSTEIN'S CRITIQUE OF REFERENTIALISM AND EXPRESSIVISM

In *Philosophical Investigations* Wittgenstein tries to imagine a purely referential language. A characteristic strategy of his philosophical method is to devise highly simplified languages—"language games" as he calls them. Here is one.

> Let us imagine a language for which the description given by Augustine is right. The language is meant to serve for communication between a builder A and an assistant B. A is building with building-stones: there are blocks, pillars, slabs and beams. B has to pass the stones, and that in the order in which A needs them. For this purpose they use a language consisting of the words "block," "pillar," "slab," "beam." A calls them out;—B brings the stone which he has learnt to bring at such-and-such a call.—Conceive of this as a complete primitive language (§2).

Wittgenstein is content to count this as a purely referential language, and imagines that the assistant learns the words ostensively, just as Augustine suggests. But almost any additional complexity forces us to recognize words that work differently.

> Let us now look at an extension of language 1). The builder's man knows by heart the series of words from one to ten. On being given the order, "Five slabs!", he goes to where the slabs are kept, says the words from one to five, takes up a slab for each word, and carries them to the builder. Here both parties use the language by speaking the words. Learning the numerals by heart will be one of the essential features of learning this language. . . .
>
> (Remark: We stressed the importance of learning the series of numerals by heart because there was no feature comparable to this in the

learning of language 1). And this shows us that by introducing numerals we have introduced an entirely different *kind* of instrument into our language.[3]

So there are no special objects to which the numbers refer. We can only understand their meaning by seeing how they are *used*.

We can make an even more significant correction of a purely referential theory of language by noting that these language games are only intelligible because Wittgenstein has told us what the builders are *doing* with the language. "Block" is a command, not a description of any sort.

Notice that Wittgenstein has not really presented any arguments here. Characteristically philosophy consists, in his view, in *showing*. It is therapy aimed at helping us escape from puzzles created by misleading mental pictures—or by the theories of other philosophers! Here he has shown us how restricted (and uninteresting) a purely referential language would have to be.

We can use Wittgenstein's attack on the notion of a "private language" in *Philosophical Investigations* to show comparable limitations on a purely expressivist language.[4] With regard to the expression of inner states such as sensations, he asks:

Could we . . . imagine a language in which a person could write down or give vocal expression to his inner experiences—his feelings, moods, and the rest—for his private use? (§243).

Wittgenstein does not mean using our existing language (such as English) to record private experiences. He is asking us to try to imagine the invention of a language for describing feelings if all that is involved is someone's attaching descriptions to the inner states. Such a language is logically impossible. The reason is that using language requires regularity, the following of rules.[5] But with no public *criteria* for knowing whether one is getting it right or not there is no difference between actually following a rule and supposing that one is following a rule.

So a purely expressivist language could never get off the ground. Language is the *ruled* use of speech, and no rules can apply in the case of private associations between signs and inner experiences. Without rules, the "word" is merely a noise (§§256–65).

How, then, is it possible to speak of inner experiences? We learn to apply terms on the basis of shared behavior. We can teach a child to say "I have a

---

3. This second game is found in Ludwig Wittgenstein, *Preliminary Studies for the 'Philosophical Investigations'* (generally known as *The Blue and Brown Books*), 2d ed. (New York: Harper & Row, 1969), 79.

4. Wittgenstein's target for this argument was actually a form of foundationalism, but I believe it is fair to use it for this purpose.

5. Note that these rules need not be explicit, merely implicit in the social conventions.

toothache" because children with toothaches tend to behave in recognizable ways. Due to the way language is interwoven with life, we can teach the rules. One night my son woke me complaining that his legs hurt. I was worried until I realized that he had the word wrong—he was scratching. "Oh, you mean they itch."

So both the descriptive and expressive aspects of language are intelligible only within language games, which involve publicly observable behavior, social conventions, and action. Language is bound up with "forms of life."

AUSTIN'S SPEECH-ACT THEORY

Wittgenstein is by all accounts an enigmatic thinker; Austin makes many similar points, but in a much more forthright manner.

Austin's mature theory developed from his recognition that there were many instances of language use that were being ignored by philosophers. These were "performative" uses, where to say something was itself to perform an action. For example, in the relevant circumstances, to say "I promise to pay you tomorrow" is *ipso facto* to make a promise.

This led Austin to distinguish between performatives and "constatives," the latter being (what philosophers thought of as) standard language used to state facts. But notice that stating facts is also *doing* something with language. This recognition led Austin to conclude that all language needed to be understood primarily in terms of what the speaker is *doing* in uttering it. The task he set himself in *How to Do Things with Words*[6] was to examine the conditions for "felicitous" speech acts—to ask what kinds of conditions need to be fulfilled for all to be well with a given speech act, or, alternatively, to ask about the sorts of flaws to which speech acts are prone.[7]

Conditions for a happy speech act can be summarized as follows: (1) Preconditions—speaker and hearer must share a common language and be free from relevant impediments to communication. (2) Primary conditions— the speaker must issue a sentence in the common language that is a conventional way of performing that kind of speech act. (3) Representative or de-

---

6. J. L. Austin, *How to Do Things with Words*, 2d ed., ed. J. O. Urmson and Marina Sbisà (Cambridge, MA: Harvard University Press, 1962).

7. Austin refers to the former as "happy" or "felicitous" speech acts and to the latter as "unhappy" or "infelicitous." This may seem an odd choice of words, but it is difficult to find any better. As we see below, "true" and "false" are not at all adequate to assess the speech act as a whole. Since language is considered here according to its use, we may be tempted to classify speech acts as "effective" or "ineffective," but this would suggest, for example, that I cannot have succeeded in *asking* someone to close the door without having succeeded in getting the person to comply. We need to distinguish, as Austin did, between the "illocutionary act"— the speech act itself, and its "perlocutionary effects"—what happens as a contingent consequence of performing the speech act.

scriptive conditions—the sentence must bear a relation to a state of affairs that is appropriate to that sort of speech act. (4) Affective or psychological conditions—the speaker must intend to perform the speech act by means of the sentence and have the relevant attitudes or affects; the hearer must take the speaker to have the requisite intentions and affects (uptake).[8]

These conditions become interesting when we consider how their proper fulfillment varies from one speech act to another. Here is a very simple example: I ask a student in class to "please close the door." For the happiness of this speech act:

1. Preconditions: The student must understand English and be able to hear me.
2. Primary conditions: "Please *x*" must be a conventional way of making a request in our language.
3. Representative conditions: There must be a door, and it must be *open;* the student must be capable of closing it.
4. Affective conditions: I must *want* the door to be closed and *intend* that my sentence be taken by the student as such a request. The student must recognize this intention by way of understanding the utterance.

Now, consider a slightly different speech act: "Thank you for closing the door."

1. (Same as above.)
2. "Thank you for *x*" must be a conventional way of expressing gratitude.
3. There must be a door; it must be *closed;* it must be the case that this student is the one who last closed it.
4. I must be grateful that the student closed the door and intend my sentence to be taken as an expression of that attitude. The student must recognize this intention by way of understanding the utterance.

The important point to notice for our purposes is that ordinarily there are both expressive and representative *dimensions* involved in every happy speech act. In the two cases above the representative dimension is essential, but it varies depending on the act in question. In the first case there needs to be an open door; in the second, a closed door. Each act requires the expression of an attitude and an intention, but here too the appropriate attitude varies depending on the type of speech act.

So reference and expression are both essential to most speech acts, but the question of the nature of the speech act—the question of what one is attempting to do with the sentence—is prior, since this determines the sorts of inner attitudes that are appropriate and determines, as well, what sort of relation there needs to be between language and the world. From this perspective, any account of language that attempts to *begin* with representation or expression is doomed to inadequacy.[9]

---

8. This is a summary of Austin's conditions worked out by McClendon and Smith in *Convictions.* We look at McClendon and Smith below.

9. "Begin" in the sense of logical priority, not temporal.

As mentioned above, Austin gave up on the distinction between language that performs an action and language that states a fact, due to recognition that stating is itself *doing* something with language.[10] Alasdair MacIntyre has an amusing example that illustrates the importance of knowing what someone is *doing* in stating a fact.

> I am standing waiting for a bus and the young man standing next to me suddenly says: "The name of the common wild duck is *Histrionicus histrionicus histrionicus.*" There is no problem as to the meaning of the sentence he uttered: the problem is to answer the question, what was he doing in uttering it? Suppose he just uttered such sentences at random intervals; this would be one possible form of madness. We would render his action of utterance intelligible if one of the following turned out to be true. He has mistaken me for someone who yesterday had approached him in the library and asked: "Do you by any chance know the Latin name of the common wild duck?" *Or* he has just come from a session with his psychotherapist who has urged him to break down his shyness by talking to strangers. "But what shall I say?" "Oh, anything at all." *Or* he is a Soviet spy waiting at a prearranged rendez-vous and uttering the ill-chosen code sentence which will identify him to his contact. In each case the act of utterance becomes intelligible by finding its place in a narrative.[11]

Once we know the kind of speech act intended we can then assess its felicity along the lines Austin has laid out. If he is answering the library patron's question:
1. and 2. (rather uninteresting).
3. It must in fact be the case that this is the name of the common wild duck.
4. He must believe this to be the case and intend his sentence to be taken as an answer to the question. And—here is where the speech act is bound to go awry—MacIntyre must take his sentence to be the answer to such an earlier question.

Alternatively, if he is a spy:
1. They do not necessarily need to speak any more English than this one sentence.
2. This will need to be a specially pre-arranged code—a convention only between the two of them and perhaps in force only for the day.
3. It need *not* be true that this is the name of the wild duck.

---

10. It is surprising that many who talk about "Austin on performative utterance" never notice that Austin gave up this distinction! George Lindbeck may be one of these; see *The Nature of Doctrine*, 65.

11. MacIntyre, *After Virtue*, 210.

4. The speaker needs to intend that MacIntyre *not* take him to be informing him of the name of the duck, but rather that MacIntyre recognize his intention to identify himself as the fellow spy; MacIntyre needs to "get it."

Because speech acts, even the simplest stating of a fact, are more complex than modern philosophers imagined, the array of criteria for assessing them must be more complex than the single criterion of truth or falsity. As we have just seen, there is a variety of ingredients that go into their assessment; some of these are conventional appropriateness or inappropriateness, ingenuousness or its opposite, accuracy or inaccuracy, fairness or unfairness. And the nature of the speech act itself determines what kinds of standards of truth apply. Sometimes "truth" is not even the appropriate judgment, as we saw in the case of the spy's secret code. One of Austin's own examples in *How to Do Things with Words* is the following:

Suppose we confront "France is hexagonal" with the facts, in this case, I suppose, with France, is it true or false? Well, if you like, up to a point; of course I can see what you mean by saying that it is true for certain intents and purposes. It is good enough for a top-ranking general, perhaps, but not for a geographer. "Naturally it is pretty rough," we should say, "and pretty good as a pretty rough statement." But then someone says: "But is true or is it false? I don't mind whether it is rough or not; of course it's rough, but it has to be true or false—it's a statement isn't it? How can one answer this question, whether it is true or false that France is hexagonal? It is just rough, and that is the right and final answer to the question of the relation of "France is hexagonal" to France. It is a rough description; it is not a true or false one (143).

CHANGING IMAGES OF LANGUAGE

Wittgenstein claims that much philosophical confusion comes from being captivated by a picture. An apt illustration is the sort of skepticism that comes from imagining a body of knowledge to be structured like a building, and then fearing that it will be left hanging in mid-air if we can find it no suitable foundation.

The image of language as a picture of reality is a similarly captivating picture, and one that beguiled Wittgenstein himself in his early years. We imagine that the sentence "The cat is on the mat" is a picture of a fact, where the cat is represented by the word *cat*, the mat by *mat*, and *on* pictures the relation between them.

What the later Wittgenstein offers in place of the "picture" picture is a *moving* picture. To understand the sentence, ask for a little story that makes sense of what a person might be *doing* with that sentence in a social setting; for example, answering a question about where to look for Tabby.

If it is the case, as Wittgenstein and Austin claim, that the "picture" picture fails to work for most language, then why have we all been so beguiled for so long?

Richard Rorty relates this picture of language to an equally long-standing picture of the human mind:

> It is pictures rather than propositions, metaphors rather than statements, which determine most of our philosophical convictions. The picture which holds traditional philosophy captive is that of the mind as a great mirror, containing various representations—some accurate, some not—and capable of being studied by pure, nonempirical methods. Without the notion of the mind as a mirror, the notion of knowledge as accuracy of representation would not have suggested itself.[12]

Instead, he argues, we would likely have developed a more pragmatic conception of knowledge. Also, without the mirror metaphor, modern philosophers would not have approached the study of language as though representing were its only function.

Rorty traces the metaphor of mind as a mirror back to Ancient Greece, pointing out that this is where *visual* images for knowledge first arise. But it is fruitless, he claims,

> to ask whether the Greek language, or Greek economic conditions, or the idle fancy of some nameless pre-Socratic, is responsible for viewing this sort of knowledge as *looking* at something (rather than, say, rubbing up against it, or crushing it underfoot, or having sexual intercourse with it) (39).

However, Walter J. Ong has done extensive research on the differences between oral and literate cultures. The picture theory of language depends on visual metaphors—thinking of words and sentences as things that can be seen. Ong believes that our emphasis on visual metaphors for language and knowledge can be traced to the development of written language.

> Oral peoples commonly think of names (one kind of words) as conveying power over things. . . . Chirographic [= writing] and typographic [= printing] folk tend to think of names as labels, written or printed tags imaginatively affixed to an object named. Oral folk have no sense of a name as a tag, for they have no idea of a name as something that can be seen.[13]

---

12. Richard Rorty, *Philosophy and the Mirror of Nature* (Princeton, NJ: Princeton University Press, 1979), 12.

13. Walter Ong, *Orality and Literacy: The Technologizing of the Word* (London and New York: Methuen, 1982), 33.

So the visual metaphors entered Western philosophical thought as a result of the transition from a purely oral culture to one whose educated class can write. But the visual, representative view of knowledge and language became commonplace only in the modern period, after the printing press allowed for widespread literacy and a thorough shift from an oral to a literate culture.

Whereas written language is associated with contemplation—inactivity— oral language is associated with action. Oral cultures tend to pay more attention to people rather than to objects.[14] This latter distinction correlates with Rorty's claim that there are two ways to think about knowledge and truth: One is in terms of "objectivity"; that is, correspondence between language and the (physical) world. The other is in terms of "solidarity"; that is, in terms of positions that all people involved in a conversation can come to accept.[15]

These reflections on the shift away from metaphors for language that see it as primarily a doing in the social world may help us to recognize that the representational view is not simply a *fact* about how language works, but rather a widely accepted *theory* derived from a set of metaphors and images, which may not provide the most enlightening or useful understanding.[16] It might also encourage us to attempt to reimage language as a form of human action and also to consider whether an understanding of language such as we find in Austin's speech-act theory can solve some of the problems that the modern representative theory created for theologians and philosophers of religion. It is the thesis of this chapter that a more adequate account will show the strengths and weaknesses of both the modern liberal expressivist theory and the modern propositional theory, while overcoming the dichotomy between these two approaches to religious language.

McCLENDON AND SMITH

McClendon and Smith have made explicit use of Austin's theory for understanding religious language. They focus especially on religious *convictions*— the deeply-held beliefs that are constitutive of the identity of a person or a religious community.

Let us see how a speech-act analysis of a religious conviction allows us to transcend the liberal-conservative debate over the nature of religious language. One kind of speech act McClendon and Smith consider is a confession of faith. Their example is a confession by a Christian or Jewish teacher named Aleph of his conviction G: "God led Israel across the Sea of Reeds." Here are their proposed conditions for the happiness of such a speech act:

---

14. Ibid., 68.

15. See especially Richard Rorty, *Contingency, Irony, and Solidarity* (Cambridge: Cambridge University Press, 1989).

16. Note the visual metaphors in this very sentence: "reflection," "see," "view," "enlightening"!

1. *Preconditions.* [Same as above.]
2. *Primary conditions.*
    2.1 The speaker issues a sentence . . . in the common language.
    2.2 There is a convention of the language to the effect that this sentence is a way of (performing the speech-act of) confessing.
We explicate 2.2 as follows:
    2.21 In issuing this sentence the speaker takes up or maintains a certain stance, to which the speaker is thereby committed.
    2.22 In issuing this sentence, the speaker displays, i.e., witnesses to, this stance.
3. *Representative or descriptive conditions.* In issuing this sentence the speaker describes or represents the relevant state(s) of affairs with sufficient exactness to make it possible for the speaker to take up that stance (2.21) and to display it (2.22).
    The relevant state(s) of affairs will vary from confession to confession. In our story, Aleph's G requires:
    3.1 In a certain historical context, a certain event (being led across the Sea of Reeds) has occurred to a certain people (Israel).
    3.2 This event is attributable to the God acknowledged in this context.
    3.3 This God exists.
4. *Affective or psychological conditions.*
    4.1 The speaker has a certain affect, namely, awed gratitude, and in issuing this sentence conveys his possession of it to the hearer.
    4.2 The speaker's intention in issuing this sentence is to use the language's convention for confession (see 2.2), and he intends the hearer to understand (by his use) that he is so using it.
    4.3 The hearer on the basis of the issued sentence takes the speaker to have the requisite affect (see 4.1) and intentions (see 4.2), and he takes the speaker to have displayed or witnessed to the stance (see 2.22 and 3).[17]

In light of this account of religious language we can see that both the expressivist and propositional theories of religious language contain partial truths, yet neither alone provides an adequate account of religious language. To "state the facts" about God without an appropriate attitude toward God is surely to have failed to get the point of what one is saying. (Similarly, to state the facts about God but to fail to live accordingly is likewise to have failed to recognize what one is saying.)

Yet to confess religious attitudes detached from any sort of factual content is to confess . . . well . . . nothing. One cannot express gratitude to God unless God has done something *for which* one is grateful, any more than I can happily thank a student for closing the door if she did not in fact close it.

---

17. McClendon and Smith, *Convictions*, 62-63.

Some contemporary theologians of the liberal type attempt to escape this problem by describing religious attitudes as attitudes toward life or reality that involve minimal propositional content, for example, David Tracy's "basic faith in the worthwhileness of existence."

McClendon and Smith point out that the condition that creates the most problems (for believers, at least) is 3.2: "This event is attributable to the God acknowledged in this context." Here, once again, we encounter the vexing problem of divine action. One common way to approach it would be the (early) conservative assumption that *supernatural* events occurred in the past and were easily recognizable to anyone present—perhaps because of their likeness to a Cecil B. DeMille movie. Another common strategy (prevalent among theologians of the liberal type) would be to claim that some unusual, but non-miraculous, event occurred (a strong wind drying the marsh land) coupled with a "faith experience" on the part of the Israelites.

Ronald Thiemann, whose work we surveyed briefly in the previous chapter, would be unhappy with the latter solution and, in his account of holist theological method, makes a suggestion that we can employ here. He argues that theology must pay attention to "criteria of judgment internal to the Christian tradition." "Theology of this kind is a critical reflective activity which seeks the norm for faith and practice not beyond but within the first-order language of the church."[18]

I have argued elsewhere that the Christian church has a practice, often called discernment, which employs a set of criteria, internal to the Christian tradition, for judging whether events are instances of divine action. The practice involves discussion and, thus, a community, even if only of two. The task is to evaluate a purported act of God; for example: Was that a prophetic utterance or not? Is this a divine healing or a purely natural event? Is it God calling me to the ministry or only my superego?

While there is some variation from one Christian community to another, the criteria tend to be similar. The following are typical:

1. Consistency of the event or utterance in question with scriptural teaching or with a scriptural pattern of life.
2. Consequences—production of the fruits of the Spirit; growth into the character of Christ; unity and strengthening of the body of Christ.
3. Circumstances—whether and how the event fits into a meaningful narrative pattern.[19]

The point of having a *communal* practice with applicable *criteria* can be seen in light of Wittgenstein's arguments against the possibility of a private, purely expressive language. There have to be *public* criteria and (at least implicit) *rules* governing the use of language (here, to govern statements such as "This event is attributable to God"), and it has to be possible to distinguish between cases where the linguistic rules have been followed and cases where

---

18. Thiemann, *Revelation and Theology*, 74, 75.
19. See Murphy, *Theology in the Age of Scientific Reasoning*, chap. 5.

they have not. Given such rules, *and their workability when woven into the life of the community,* Christians in the relevant community are *so far* justified in attributing divine influence to events that have passed the test.

So communal discernment is an instance of Thiemann's employment of criteria of judgment internal to the Christian tradition in order to regulate the first-order language of the church. However, McClendon and Smith point out that there is a further requirement for the happiness of a speech act involving divine action: some resolution needs to be provided of the clash between the traditional Jewish and Christian conviction that God is an agent in history and the modern scientific conviction that the universe is a closed causal order. In their case this is expressed in condition 3.3, "This God [the God who acts in history] exists." We take up this issue in Chapter 6.

A final requirement highlighted by McClendon and Smith for the happiness of Aleph's confession arises because of the necessary connection between a person's attitudes and behavior. How do we know that Aleph does in fact possess the proper attitude of "awed gratitude"? Here, again, there must be public criteria; it is not sufficient for Aleph merely to suppose he is grateful. The public criteria involve *acting* in such a way as to reflect gratitude and awe.

So we come back, again, to the Wittgensteinian and Austinian point that language is not *about* the world, a reflection of reality, but is *in* the world, and its appropriateness, efficacy, truth, and the like are a matter of how it comports with the actual living of life.

AUSTINIAN REFLECTIONS ON BIBLICAL INTERPRETATION

In this section I propose that we consider the light that may be shed on the understanding of scriptural interpretation by a speech-act theory of language. That is, let us take the texts to be analogous to speech acts (or, rather, to complex collections of speech acts and "editorial acts") as opposed to either (mere) expressions of religious awareness or (mere) factual accounts.

For these purposes I shall summarize Austin's conditions for a happy speech act somewhat differently than did McClendon and Smith. I suggest that we distinguish five dimensions, or kinds of conditions, that need to be considered in understanding and assessing a speech act:

1. linguistic conventions;
2. social conventions;
3. referential conditions;
4. expressivist or psychological conditions;
5. uptake.

Given this list, we can see that a variety of types of biblical criticism aim at understanding the texts by investigating *one* of these five dimensions. Traditional syntactic and semantic studies (investigations of grammar and word use) aim at bringing it about that writer and reader share a common language. That is, we need to come to understand the *linguistic conventions* of the writer (or editor).

Form criticism aims at recognizing literary units, which the authors have incorporated into their texts, such as laws, priestly instructions, prophetic oracles, hymns, poems, prayers, confessions of faith, miracle stories. Put in Austinian terms, the form critic studies the *social conventions* of the Ancient Hebrew or New Testament communities in order to recognize the use—the type of speech act—that a selected passage constituted in its original setting. It is important to recognize that there are "layers" of speech acts in the Scriptures. For example, Galatians 3:28, "There is no longer Jew or Greek, there is no longer slave or free, there is no longer male and female; for all of you are one in Christ Jesus," is thought to be an early baptismal formula. However, Paul is *using* it here to celebrate God's great promise, available through faith to all alike. Genre criticism can also be seen as the attempt to recover the social conventions within which a text or passage functioned in its day.

Historical criticism can be understood as an attempt to examine the felicity of biblical speech acts with regard to their referential dimension: *was* there a people called the Hebrews or the Habiru, who migrated from Egypt into the land of Canaan?

It is important to notice that the kind of speech act involved governs the kind of fit required between text and history. For example, consider Hans Frei's suggestion about the purpose of the Gospel narratives. Frei claims that the *force* of the Gospels is to provide identity descriptions—stories to render a character. Their purpose is to say: this risen Christ whom you know as present to you in worship is in fact Jesus of Nazareth, who was born . . . taught . . . suffered and died.[20]

The referential conditions for a speech act of this sort include the background condition (1) that the readers must have in fact known the presence of the risen Christ. The more immediate conditions that must be fulfilled for the success of the gospel stories as speech acts are: (2) The narrative must serve to identify one specific individual—and for this certain historical facts needed to be true—enough facts to distinguish Jesus from any other similar character. We might include here the identity of his parents, his home town, the outlines of his public ministry, and the circumstances of his death. (3) The stories of his teaching and actions must be truly *characteristic* of him; that is, they must have presented an accurate portrait of his character. Notice that truth-*likeness* is at least as important here as objective historical accuracy. In fact, we can sometimes render a character more accurately by means of characteristic stories about what the person might have done than by recounting less revealing specific incidents.

Contrast the force of the Gospels, now, with Paul's preaching of the resurrection. Here Paul was addressing communities in which some still lived

---

20. Hans Frei, *The Identity of Jesus Christ: The Hermeneutical Bases of Dogmatic Theology* (Philadelphia: Fortress Press, 1975).

who had known Jesus in the flesh. The force of Paul's speech acts is to proclaim that this well-known historical figure has been raised. The representative conditions here are reordered. As a background condition there must have been a historical Jesus known to those present by acquaintance or testimony, and this condition we can easily assume to have been fulfilled. The more immediate and interesting condition is that there must have been some peculiar event involving the body of that well-known figure that could reasonably have been described by the metaphorical term *resurrection*. But since such an event could not have been directly observable, the most that could be asked was that a sufficient number of hearers have access to enough evidence to be able reasonably to accept Paul's testimony. So we see that the particularities of audience and intended *force* of the documents determine what will *count* as fulfilling the representative (historical) conditions.

Some hermeneutical theories, beginning at least as early as the work of Friedrich Schleiermacher, have sought the meaning of the text in the mind (the intentions) of the author. For Schleiermacher, one goal of interpretation was to enter imaginatively and sympathetically into the author's religious consciousness, reliving and rethinking the author's thoughts and feelings. However, many today would deny the possibility of recovering the author's mental states, and some would add that for the purposes of interpretation these intentions would be of no interest even if they could be recovered.

A speech-act approach to biblical interpretation would side with Schleiermacher in claiming that it is necessary to understand the author's intention. One condition for a happy speech act is uptake, which involves understanding what the author intended to do by means of the passage in question. However, the recognition of authorial intent does not require imagination and empathy so much as knowledge of the linguistic and social conventions of the author's time. Unless we suppose for whatever reason that the author was dishonest or incompetent in using the language, then we do have public access to what the author intended. There is no hidden mental component—the intention or the meaning—to be sought beyond the (written) speech act itself. So it is true *in a sense* that we can never recover the mind of the author—it is true in the trivial sense that we never have immediate access to anyone's thoughts but our own. But it is obviously false in another sense, since in the normal, "happy" state of affairs, people's speech acts are, exactly, public enactments of their intentions.[21]

Finally, a new entry in the biblical critic's list of approaches is reader-response criticism. This is an understanding of the understanding of texts borrowed from contemporary literary critics such as Stanley Fish.

Stanley Fish has had considerable influence on biblical scholars. I believe a survey of his earlier and later works will serve to illustrate two poles of the spectrum of reader-response theories. Thus, I shall distinguish between the early Fish and the later Fish. The early Fish parallels the deconstructionists

---

21. Cf. McClendon and Smith, *Convictions*, 43.

and other radical critics in that he seems to suggest that the meaning of a text is nothing but the effect it has on the individual reader. The later Fish will turn out be an ally of Austin and McClendon and Smith.[22]

Fish began by focusing on the question, what does this word (sentence, play, poem) do? In the sequence from writer to text to reader, meaning only "happens" when the text has an effect on the reader: "There is no direct relation between the meaning of a sentence (paragraph, novel, poem) and what its words mean. . . . It is the experience of an utterance . . . that *is* the meaning."[23]

The sort of effect the early Fish sought to understand can be illustrated by his analysis of the following sentence:

That Judas perished by hanging himself, there is no certainty in Scripture: though in one place it seems to affirm it, and by a doubtful word hath given occasion to translate it; yet in another place, in a more punctual description, it maketh it improbable, and seems to overthrow it.[24]

Fish points out that the first clause is understood to be shorthand for "the *fact* that Judas perished by hanging himself." So the reader is set up to expect that the rest of the sentence will follow from this positive assertion, and thus "there is not . . ." ought to be followed by "doubt" rather than "certainty." The rest of the sentence, step by step, frustrates the expectation set up in the first clause, progressively disorientating the reader. So the sort of response with which Fish is concerned here is psychological: frustration, confusion, and the like.

However, the later Fish is concerned with genuine Austinian uptake. In "Is There a Text in This Class?" he concentrates on *understanding* texts and emphasizes the shared *conventions* that make it possible for reader or listener to "get it."[25] Here his illustration is an anecdote:

On the first day of the new semester a colleague at Johns Hopkins University was approached by a student who, as it turned out, had just taken a course from me. She put to him what I think you would agree is a perfectly straightforward question. "Is there a text in this class?" Responding with a confidence so perfect that he was unaware of it . . . my colleague said, "Yes, it's the *Norton Anthology of Literature*," whereupon the trap (set not by the student but by the infinite capacity

22. This notwithstanding Fish's claims about what one *cannot* do with speech-act theory. See "How to Do Things with Austin and Searle," in *Is There a Text in This Class?* (Cambridge, MA: Harvard University Press, 1980), 197-245.

23. Stanley Fish, "Literature in the Reader: Affective Stylistics," in Fish, *Is There a Text in This Class?*, 21-67; quotation, 32.

24. Fish, "Literature in the Reader," 23.

25. In Fish, *Is There a Text in This Class?*, 303-21.

of language for being appropriated) was sprung: "No, no," she said, "I mean in this class do we believe in poems and things, or is it just us?" (305).

While Fish uses the anecdote to illustrate his claims regarding the "instability of the text" and the "unavailability of determinate meanings," he argues here, against the supposed implication that texts can mean anything we want, that the possibilities for different interpretations are in fact sharply limited by the practices and assumptions that make up the text's social context. This anecdote is interesting just because it is an unusual case where two such contexts were available. One is the general rubric "first day of class," which makes the first meaning available; the second becomes available only within the narrower context of "Fish's victims." Both interpretations were a function of public and constituting norms of language and understanding. In most instances there is in fact only one such context available (and this is what has allowed earlier theorists to overlook the role of social conventions).

So the later Fish still maintains that reader-response is what constitutes the meaning of the text, but argues for the necessity of *social conventions* to enable uptake; he recognizes as well that these same conventions (ordinarily) enable the reader or listener to reach correct understanding of the writer's or speaker's *intention* and of the intended *reference*. We could say that the later Fish's point is that neither linguistic conventions nor referent nor intention alone is sufficient to establish meaning. Social conventions must be considered as well. We can make a parallel claim regarding biblical interpretation: neither word studies, nor form and genre criticism, nor historical criticism alone will enable readers to get the point of a scriptural passage (and in so doing to recognize the author's or editor's intention). Rather, all of these dimensions must come together in answering the question, what is this text *doing*?[26]

Having now exhibited some of the complexity involved in applying Austin's speech-act account to the interpretation of biblical texts, I wish to suggest an analogy. Wittgenstein devised simplified "language games" in order to draw our attention to features of *real* language games. Rather than say a biblical text *is* a speech act, and these are its conditions for happiness, we might rather say that an Austinian speech act is to a biblical text as one of Wittgenstein's simplified language games is to language use in all its complexity. Then we can think of Austin's speech-act analysis not as a complete theory of biblical language, but rather as pointing us in the right directions to recognize the kinds of factors that must be considered for an adequate understanding of biblical language. To understand Austin's theory is to be able to start with it and then to go on to more complex cases.

---

26. This argument is from my "Textual Relativism, Philosophy of Language, and the baptist Vision," in Hauerwas, et al., *Theology without Foundations*.

GEORGE LINDBECK'S CULTURAL-LINGUISTIC THEORY

Lindbeck's recommendation for postliberal theology (which he says might be called postmodern as well) grows out of a "cultural-linguistic" understanding of religion borrowed from the social sciences. This view emphasizes the respects in which religions resemble cultures or languages together with their correlative forms of life. Religions are understood as idioms for the construing of reality and the living of life. In such a scheme, doctrines are best treated as second-order discourse—as rules to guide both practice and the use of first-order religious language (praise, preaching, exhortation, and the like).

Notice the Austinian feature: Lindbeck's first question about doctrines is, what do they *do?* The recognition of the inextricability of language from life recalls the work of both Austin and Wittgenstein.

Lindbeck contrasts his cultural-linguistic view of religion and its "regulative" theory of doctrine with the two older theories with which we were concerned in the first chapters of this book; he calls them the cognitive-propositional and experiential-expressivist theories.

Lindbeck's cultural-linguistic view does not ignore the cognitive or experiential dimensions of religions; rather, he claims that the linguistic categories and grammar provided by the religion are necessary *conditions* for both cognition and experience. A religion is a communal phenomenon that shapes the subjectivities of individuals rather than being primarily a manifestation of those subjectivities. It is a linguistic medium that *makes possible* the description of realities and the formation of beliefs, rather than being a catalogue of those beliefs.

We saw in the previous chapter that the question of truth arises in three ways in a cultural-linguistic approach. One question concerns the consistency or coherence of each part of the system with the rest—first-order community practices and beliefs must be consistent with second-order theological and doctrinal statements, and vice versa. Such consistency measurements are intrasystemic or "intratextual." Second, one must raise a question about the adequacy of the concepts, the sufficiency of the linguistic resources provided. Finally, one may raise a question about the "truth" of the religion itself, but this is better expressed as a question about the adequacy of the system as a whole to conform its adherents in the various dimensions of their existence to what is "Ultimately Real."

Hans Frei has written that Lindbeck's *Nature of Doctrine* will receive "plenty of flak," and that this will come more from the propositionalists than from the experiential-expressivists.

There will be moderate propositionalists who will tell him that what he says about doctrines as second-order rules is sufficiently kin to doctrines as first-order propositional statements that he could allow second-order doctrines about the Trinity, atonement, etc., to have the character not only of intra-systematic truth but ontological truth statements. Would he please say more on that score?[27]

Frei confesses, "half under [his] breath," to "some *qualified* sympathy for the moderate propositionalists" (279).

I am sure that many readers of Lindbeck's slim volume were hoping for a more substantial work to follow, which would spell out his views in greater detail and address criticisms and questions such as those to which Frei alludes. In the absence of such a volume, I shall undertake a few comments.

David Kelsey summarizes Lindbeck's position in terms of a chain of metaphors and a final analogy: "A religion (in this case, Christianity) is (like) a culture; a culture is (like) a language; and as French grammar is to the French language, so is Christian doctrine to Christianity."[28]

> Lindbeck proposes that the "abiding and doctrinally significant" aspect of Christianity lies "in the story it tells" (a story which functions as an "idiom" for Christians) "and in the grammar that informs the way the story is told and used." This story, as narrated in canonical Scriptures, is the source of "the core of lexical elements" in this language (symbols, concepts, rites, injunctions, stories); but it is the "grammar" of Christianity, not the lexicon, "which church doctrines chiefly reflect" (9).

Let us see now what answer can be made on Lindbeck's behalf to the moderate propositionalist, who asks whether, despite their regulative function, doctrines do not also involve some propositional content. To do so, we shall have to take a detour through some recent analytic philosophy.

In the previous chapter I described the emergence and then the demise of a view of philosophy that saw itself as capable of attaining universal and incorrigible knowledge by restricting its purview to the conceptual ingredient in knowledge while leaving the "empirical content" to science. The universality and incorrigibility were soon recognized (by many) to be false hopes, because (on the basis of *empirical* study of other cultures!) it turns out that there is a variety of conceptual schemes in existence (so much for the universality)[29] and our own conceptual scheme is regularly "warped" to accommodate new empirical discoveries or for the sake of simplification (so much for

---

27. Hans Frei, "Epilogue: George Lindbeck and *The Nature of Doctrine*," in *Theology and Dialogue: Essays in Conversation with George Lindbeck*, ed. Bruce D. Marshall (Notre Dame: University of Notre Dame Press, 1990), 275-82; quotation, 278.

28. David Kelsey, "Church Discourse and Public Realm," in Marshall, *Theology and Dialogue*, 7-33; quotation, 8.

29. One account of the multiplicity of conceptual schemes embodied in different linguistic systems is that of Benjamin Lee Whorf. I am particularly impressed by his account of radically different concepts of time and place among the Hopi Indians. See *Language, Thought, and Reality: Selected Writings of Benjamin Lee Whorf*,

incorrigibility).[30] In short, we can make only a rough distinction between the categories or *concepts* we have available for our use in thinking and speaking and the *content* of the claims we make using those conceptual resources.

Stephan Körner has shed some light on this issue in his development of the concept of a *categorial framework*. Specifying a categorial framework involves listing all of the maximal categories—the major classifications—that are needed for construing reality, along with their subordinate genera and the criteria for membership in those categories. It also involves stating the logical assumptions to be employed in reasoning.

Körner's categorial framework is but a more formal account of what Lindbeck and Kelsey are calling a "lexicon" or "idiom" together with a "grammar." What is important for our purposes is Körner's claim that a categorial framework necessarily involves claims about the nature of reality.

> The manner in which a person classifies the objects of his experience into highest classes or categories, the standards of intelligibility which he applies, and the metaphysical beliefs which he holds are intimately related. To give an obvious example, the employment of the category of causally determined events, the demand that all or some explanations be causal, and the belief that nature is at least partly a deterministic system so involve each other that they are either all present in a person's thinking or else all absent from it. Groups of persons, societies, and whole civilizations exhibit, in so far as they can be said to think, a similar correlation between their categories, standards of intelligibility and metaphysical beliefs.[31]

Körner's point is that to possess a category, a lexical item, such as *cause*, commits a community to certain propositions about reality; for example, that nature is at least partly a determinate system. This is due simply to the "grammar" governing the relations among the concepts, to logic, and to the rules for what count as instances of the concepts.

---

ed. John B. Carroll (Cambridge, MA: MIT Press, 1956). See also Paul Feyerabend on the incommensurable conceptual schemes of archaic and classical Greece in *Against Method*, 1st ed. (London: New Left Books, 1975), chap. 17. This material does not appear in the revised editions.

I do not agree with Donald Davidson's dismissal of the notion of different conceptual schemes ("On the Very Idea of a Conceptual Scheme," in *Proceedings and Addresses of the American Philosophical Association* 47 [1973-74]: 5-20); see Nancey Murphy, "Theology in the Age of Probable Reasoning," dissertation, Graduate Theological Union, 1987, chap. 1.

30. This is one of the consequences of Quine's truth-meaning holism. See "Two Dogmas of Empiricism." See also Wittgenstein, *Philosophical Investigations*, §xii.

31. Stephan Körner, *Categorial Frameworks* (Oxford: Basil Blackwell, 1970), ix.

Körner describes such metaphysical claims as "internally incorrigible," that is, necessarily true so long as the categorial framework is not changed. We can produce an example from a Christian categorial framework by re-describing Anselm's ontological argument in Körner's terminology: *God* is a maximal category of the Christian categorial framework. The criterion for membership in this category is being "that than which none greater can be conceived." Objects that exist independently of thought are greater than those that are merely objects of thought (this is a part of the grammar of words such as *object, reality,* and *existence* in Anselm's day). Therefore, the statement "God exists" is internally incorrigible. However, such claims are externally corrigible—they may appear unintelligible, questionable, or obviously false from the point of view of a different categorial framework.

My point here is to argue that doctrines conceived as grammatical rules governing the use of the Christian conceptual scheme cannot fail to entail or presuppose beliefs about reality. In other words, doctrines by their very nature *as rules* carry propositional content. This is part of my answer, on Lindbeck's behalf, to Frei's moderate propositionalists.

However, Frei's imagined interlocutors were asking not only about intrasystematic truth (that is, internal incorrigibility), but ontological truth. Here it is appropriate to refer the reader (once again) to MacIntyre's account of *external* justification of the entire tradition, with its stories, lexicon, grammar, and entailed ontological claims.[32]

An intriguing consequence of Lindbeck's conception of religious language is his account of how to read the Bible. Until recently, he claims, Christians "dwelt imaginatively in the biblical world."[33] This is no longer the case, due to two factors. One is simply the decline in "biblical literacy"—even devout Christians do not know the texts well enough to be shaped by them. Another factor is that

> modernity has been deeply prejudiced against treating a classic as a language or lens with many meanings or uses with which to construe reality and view the world. Instead . . . modernity viewed texts primarily as objects of study (50).

In other words, rather than using the texts to interpret life, moderns have taken to interpreting the text, trying to make sense of *it* in terms of their own modern categories.

---

32. See "Against Relativism" in chap. 4 above; MacIntyre, *Three Rival Versions of Moral Enquiry*; and idem, *Whose Justice? Which Rationality?*, esp. chaps. 1, 10, and 18.

33. George Lindbeck, "The Church's Mission to a Postmodern Culture," in *Postmodern Theology: Christian Faith in a Pluralist World,* ed. Frederic B. Burnham (San Francisco: HarperSanFrancisco, 1989), 37-55; quotation, 42.

Lindbeck's prescription is to reverse this modern turn by reviving biblical literacy.

This literacy does not consist of historical, critical knowledge about the Bible. Nor does it consist of theological accounts, couched in nonbiblical language, of the Bible's teachings and meanings. Rather it is the patterns and details of its sagas and stories, its images and symbols, its syntax and grammar, which need to be internalized if one is to imagine and think scripturally (51-52).

A postmodern interpretation of Scripture seeks not to redescribe biblical realities in contemporary concepts, but rather to allow the texts themselves to "absorb the universe." It is the Bible that ought to supply "the interpretive framework with which believers seek to live their lives and understand reality."[34]

It is important to note the direction of interpretation. Typology does not make scriptural contents into metaphors for extrascriptural realities, but the other way around. It does not suggest, as is often said in our day, that believers find their stories in the Bible, but rather that they make the story of the Bible their story. The cross is not to be viewed as a figurative representation of suffering nor the messianic kingdom as a symbol for hope in the future; rather, suffering should be cruciform, and the hopes for the future messianic.[35]

In Chapter 4 we saw that MacIntyre understands a tradition as an ongoing, socially embodied argument about how best to interpret and apply the community's formative texts. So here Lindbeck is making an important argument regarding interpretation. In short, proper interpretation *is* application.

A TEST CASE: DONALD BLOESCH

In Chapter 2 I classified Donald Bloesch as a propositionalist with regard to his theory of language. However, I was struck in reading his somewhat labored attempts to describe biblical language by the fact that he very easily could make the points he wants to make with an Austinian theory of language.

Bloesch says that God's self-disclosure in revelation is both conceptual and existential.

Even the propositions of the Bible are not yet revelation when they are only comprehended as cognitive assertions. Revelation is indeed cognitive, but it is much more than this. It is an act of communication by

---

34. Lindbeck, *The Nature of Doctrine*, 117.
35. Ibid., 118.

which God confronts the whole person with his redeeming mercy and glorious presence. It therefore involves not only the mind but also the will and affections.[36]

While Bloesch is speaking specifically of biblical language here, rather than speech acts of Christians, it clearly follows that any speech acts in response to the biblical revelation must involve appropriate affect (such as McClendon's and Smith's awed gratitude) and the effects on the will of the one who responds must be evidenced in suitable action.

Most interesting is Bloesch's position on myth. In response to Rudolf Bultmann he argues that while the Bible does employ mythic language, its point is theological not anthropological: "The mythopoetic imagery of the Bible is not the projection of inner experiences on the plane of history but a vehicle by which the objective intrusion of God into history is described" (266). These divine acts are not describable in literal, univocal language. So mythical and figurative language together provide the only possible medium for speaking about such events.

Bloesch describes the biblical authors' strategy as the "mythicization of history" as well as the "historicization of myth." What this means is that "the biblical authors often began with the historical facts and then added mythological allusions, thus giving the facts more than simply historical significance" (262-63).

> I affirm a hermeneutic of biblical realism as opposed to a hermeneutic of literalism on the one hand and a hermeneutic of expressivism on the other. Our goal is to explicate the meaning of a revelation that objectively took place in real history but was not generally intended to transmit exact history. But neither were the biblical texts intended as symbolic objectivizations of emotional responses, as in symbolist theology (274).

Let us see now whether we can make Bloesch's points in Austinian language: The kind of speech act involved in the texts to which Bloesch refers is an account of God's acts in history, as opposed to mere historical reporting or to reporting the writers' faith experiences. However, there are no ready-made conventional forms for speech acts of this sort, so the biblical writers created forms by weaving mythic elements (which are conventional forms generally used for other purposes) into their historical narratives. The conditions for the happiness of these speech acts can be summarized as follows:

1. a common language;
2. the *creation* of conventional "mythopoetic" forms, which can be recognized as such by the relevant community;

---

36. Bloesch, *Holy Scripture*, 48.

3. objective divine acts in history;
4. the intention on the part of the biblical writers to describe God's self-disclosure through objective acts in history; and (we can assume) the relevant attitude of faith on the part of the authors;
5. uptake—the contemporary Christian community needs "a hermeneutic of biblical realism," meaning that contemporary Christians need to recognize all of the above.

I believe that these conditions effectively summarize Bloesch's position on biblical language. I suggest that this provides some evidence that Austin's theory is a more adequate account of language than the two modern theories Bloesch had at his disposal.

A parting remark: we see once again that the question of how to understand religious language turns out to depend significantly on the issue of divine action.

CONCLUSION

This chapter ends as it began, with Wittgenstein's quotation from Augustine but with the inclusion (italicized) of a sentence omitted earlier:

> When they (my elders) named some object, and accordingly moved towards something, I saw this and I grasped that the thing was called by the sound they uttered when they meant to point it out. *Their intention was shewn by their bodily movements, as it were the natural language of all peoples: the expressions of the face, the play of the eyes, the movement of other parts of the body, and the tone of voice which expresses our state of mind in seeking, having, rejecting, or avoiding something.* Thus, as I heard words repeatedly used in their proper places in various sentences, I gradually learnt to understand what objects they signified; and after I had trained my mouth to form these signs, I used them to express my own desires. (*Confessions,* I, 8.)

Why, the reader rightly objects, the tedious repetition of this passage? The answer is that I hope that readers of this chapter will, by now, have experienced a paradigm shift in their theories of language, a Gestalt switch enabling them to recognize language as a kind of doing rather than (merely) a kind of labeling or picturing. As a result of such a shift, the account in this passage of the ostensive definition of words fades into the background, and what comes to the fore is the *action*, both linguistic and bodily. I hope it now strikes the reader as a passage not so much about affixing labels to objects, but rather about speech acts and human interactions: teaching, learning, requesting.

The task of this chapter has been to introduce an Anglo-American postmodern understanding of language and to *induce* the paradigm shift that it requires. I have claimed repeatedly that an approach to language such as that of Wittgenstein or Austin has important implications about the relation between happy use of religious language and the issue of divine action. I close with the observation that such an understanding has equally important implications for the actions of Christians. Philosophical theology (in this case, study of the nature of religious language) cannot be isolated from either the doctrine or the practices of the church.

6

Metaphysical Holism
and Divine Action

INTRODUCTION

In Chapter 3 we considered A. H. Strong's claim that miracles are at once special, extraordinary acts of God and explainable in terms of natural causes.

> A miracle is an event in nature, so extraordinary in itself and so coinciding with the prophecy or command of a religious teacher or leader, as fully to warrant the conviction, on the part of those who witness it, that God has wrought it with the design of certifying that this teacher or leader has been commissioned by him.
> This definition has certain marked advantages. . . . (a) It recognizes the immanence of God and his immediate agency in nature, instead of assuming an antithesis between the laws of nature and the will of God. (b) It regards the miracle as simply an extraordinary act of that same God who is already present in all natural operations and who in them is revealing his general plan. (c) It holds that natural law, as the method of God's regular activity, in no way precludes unique exertions of this power when these will best secure his purpose in creation. (d) It leaves it possible that all miracles may have their natural explanations and may hereafter be traced to natural causes, while both miracles and their natural causes may be only names for the one and self-same will of God. (e) It reconciles the claims of both science and religion: of science, by permitting any possible or probable physical antecedents of the miracle; of religion, by maintaining that these very antecedents together with the miracle itself are to be interpreted as signs of God's special commission to him under whose teaching or leadership the miracle is wrought.[1]

---

1. Strong, *Systematic Theology*, 188-89.

135

Against the background of the modern reductionist-determinist worldview, this combination of claims appears insupportable. It is the task of this chapter to examine changes in science and philosophy that amount to the discrediting of that reductionist worldview. Against the background of this change we can begin to see how strong claims about special divine acts may in fact be compatible with science. If science is to be credited (or blamed) for the development of the related complex of assumptions about reality that I have designated as atomism-reductionism-determinism, then it is appropriate that we turn to science for a new outlook on the basic structure of reality.

THE HIERARCHY OF THE SCIENCES REVISITED

In Chapter 3 we saw that in the modern period the sciences came to be viewed as hierarchically ordered; higher sciences study more complex systems composed of the entities studied at the next level downward. The hierarchy thus begins at the bottom with physics, then includes in order chemistry, biology, psychology (understood as the study of the behavior of complete individual organisms), then sociology. Today we might want to add ecology and cosmology, although the organization becomes problematic at these higher levels.[2] The goal of the reductionist program was to explain the behavior of entities at higher levels in terms of their parts, and ultimately in terms of physics.

However, beginning in this century there has been a different way of conceiving this same hierarchy—a nonreductionist view. Roy Wood Sellars (1880-1973) developed a position variously called emergent realism, emergent naturalism, or evolutionary naturalism; a more common term today, and the one I shall employ in this chapter, is *nonreductive physicalism.*[3] Sellars began in 1916 to explicate a conception of the mental as an emergent property in the hierarchy of complex systems,[4] and ultimately developed a conception of nature as forming a nonreducible hierarchy of levels.

Sellars's position is expressly opposed to three competitors: Cartesian mind-matter dualism; absolute idealism (the view that the mental and its

---

2. I have suggested that one has to imagine the hierarchy branching above biology, with one branch given over to the human sciences, including psychology and the social sciences, and the other to the natural sciences dealing with increasingly comprehensive systems, including ecology and cosmology. See Nancey Murphy, "Evidence of Design in the Fine-Tuning of the Universe," in Russell, Murphy, and Isham, *Quantum Cosmology and the Laws of Nature,* 407-35.

3. This term has the advantage both of being widely recognized in contemporary philosophy of mind and also, for Christians, of avoiding the atheistic connotations of *naturalism* and *materialism.*

4. See Roy W. Sellars, *Critical Realism: A Study of the Nature and Conditions of Knowledge* (New York: Russell and Russell, 1966). First published in 1916.

products are the only reality); and reductive materialism, as he designates the logical positivists' program for the unification of the sciences, that is, for the reduction of all sciences to physics.

According to Sellars, the natural world is one great complex system displaying levels of complexity that have emerged over time. In this regard he agrees with the reductive materialists as against the idealists and dualists. However, he criticizes the reductionists for having a view of nature that is overly mechanistic and atomistic. "The ontological imagination was stultified at the start by [the picture] of microscopic billiard balls."[5]

In rejecting this reductive materialism, Sellars argues that "organization and wholes are genuinely significant"; they are not mere aggregates of elementary particles. Reductive materialism overemphasizes the "stuff" in contrast to the organization. But matter is only a part of a material system. "There is energy; there is the fact of pattern; there are all sorts of intimate relations." "Matter, or stuff, needs to be supplemented by terms like integration, pattern, function."[6]

It will be my argument that science and philosophy are only now becoming sufficiently aware of the principles involved in the facts of levels, of natural kinds, of organization, to all of which the old materialism was blind. I shall even carry the notion of levels into causality and speak of *levels of causality.*[7]

The levels that Sellars countenances are the inorganic, the organic, the mental or conscious, the social, the ethical, and the spiritual. This means, he says, that ethics and sociology are each a part of the hierarchy of the sciences.[8]

Sellars argues that the mind should not be conceived as an entity, but rather as a function of the complex human organism, including its nervous system. We shall return to discuss this view and its relation to theology.

Despite Sellars's belief that science and philosophy were already in his day becoming adequately aware of the facts of levels and natural kinds, there are still a large number of ardent reductionists, and theirs has been by

---

5. Roy W. Sellars, *The Philosophy of Physical Realism* (New York: Russell and Russell, 1966), 5. First published in 1932.

6. *Principles of Emergent Realism: The Philosophical Essays of Roy Wood Sellars*, ed. W. Preston Warren (St. Louis, MO: Warren H. Green, Inc., 1970), 136-38.

7. Sellars, *The Philosophy of Physical Realism*, 4.

8. I would argue that Sellars's accounts of both ethics and religion or theology are reductive, since he bases them solely on human attitudes and values; unfortunately, his realism does not extend to God. See Nancey Murphy and George F. R. Ellis, *On the Moral Nature of the Universe: Theology, Cosmology, and Ethics* (Minneapolis: Fortress Press, 1996) for a nonreductive account of theology and ethics in the hierarchy of the sciences.

far the predominant position in philosophy and science up till the present.[9] However, I believe that the balance is beginning to shift from reductive to nonreductive physicalism.[10] And I predict that nonreductive physicalism will win the day; this is for two reasons, one scientific, the other philosophical.

At the beginning of the reductionist era, reductionists *predicted* that all science would one day reduce to physics. Their opponents argued that this would never be the case. Neither side could produce a conclusive argument. However, as the decades have gone by, evidence relevant to this controversy has accumulated. Despite astounding scientific advances brought about by means of reductive thinking, there is also growing scientific evidence for the nonreducibility of higher levels. We look first at this evidence, and then at developments in philosophical concepts that suggest that *in certain respects* total reduction is impossible in principle.

SCIENTIFIC DEVELOPMENTS

It is now becoming widely recognized by scientists working at a variety of levels in the hierarchy of the sciences that while analysis and reduction are important aspects of scientific enquiry, they do not yield a complete or adequate account of the natural world. In simple terms, one has to consider not only the parts of an entity but also its interactions with its environment in order to understand it. Since the entity plus its environment is a more complex system than the entity itself (and therefore higher in the hierarchical ordering of systems), this means that a "top-down" analysis must be considered in addition to a "bottom-up" analysis.

Science writer Silvan Schweber claims that recognition of the failure of the reductionist program has contributed to a crisis in physical theory:

> A deep sense of unease permeates the physical sciences. We are in a time of great change. . . . The underlying assumptions of physics research have shifted. Traditionally, physics has been highly reductionist, analyzing nature in terms of smaller and smaller building blocks and revealing underlying, unifying fundamental laws. In the past this grand vision has bound the subdisciplines together. Now, however,

---

9. See, for example, Hartry Field, "Physicalism," in *Inference, Explanation, and Other Frustrations: Essays in the Philosophy of Science*, ed. John Earman (Berkeley, CA: University of California Press, 1992), 271-91.

10. An effective current proponent of this nonreductive view is Arthur Peacocke. See especially his *Theology for a Scientific Age*, 2d enl. ed. (Minneapolis: Fortress Press, 1993). Besides advocating a nonreductive account of science, Peacocke also advocates "critical realism," although his position concerns theoretical entities while Sellars was concerned with objects of perception. Despite the striking parallels, I have found no references to Sellars in Peacocke's writings.

the reductionist approach that has been the hallmark of theoretical physics in the 20th century is being superseded by the investigation of emergent phenomena. . . .

The conceptual dimension of the crisis has its roots in the seeming failure of the reductionist approach, in particular its difficulties accounting for the existence of objective emergent properties.[11]

This demise of reductionism within physics itself can be attributed to the recognition of several related features of the relations among levels of analysis in science: emergence, decoupling, and top-down causation.

Emergence or *emergent order* refers to the appearance of properties and processes that are only describable by means of concepts pertaining to a higher level of analysis. New levels of order appear as biological history unfolds that require new levels of description. Neil A. Campbell describes the emergence of complexity in biology as follows:

With each step upward in the hierarchy of biological order, novel properties emerge that were not present at the simpler levels of organization. These emergent properties result from interactions between components. A molecule such as a protein has attributes not exhibited by any of its component atoms, and a cell is certainly much more than a bag of molecules. If the intricate organization of the human brain is disrupted by a head injury, that organ ceases to function properly even though all of its parts may still be present. And an organism is a living whole greater than the sum of its parts.[12]

The new concepts needed to describe the emergent properties are neither applicable at the lower level nor reducible to (translatable into) concepts at the lower level. The irreducibility of concepts entails the irreducibility of laws. Thus, many say that there are "emergent laws" at higher levels of the hierarchy.

Decoupling is a technical term in physics, but it can be used more loosely to describe the relative autonomy of levels in the hierarchy of the sciences. Schweber writes:

The ideas of symmetry breaking, the renormalization group and decoupling suggest a picture of the physical world that is hierarchically layered into quasiautonomous domains, with the ontology and dynamics of each layer essentially quasistable [i.e., largely stable] and virtually immune to whatever happens in other layers (36).

---

11. Silvan S. Schweber, "Physics, Community and the Crisis in Physical Theory," *Physics Today* (November 1993): 34-40; quotations 34, 39.

12. Neil A. Campbell, *Biology*, 2d ed. (Redwood City: Benjamin/Cummings, 1990), 2.

In other words, the causal connections among levels in the hierarchy of complexity are being called into question in two ways. There are some changes at the micro-level that make no difference at the macro-level. A familiar example is the behavior of a gas in a container. Some average properties of the gas particles (the micro-level) matter for purposes of description at the macro-level—average kinetic energy of the molecules is proportional to the absolute temperature of the gas, and the change in momentum of the gas molecules colliding with the walls of the container is related to the pressure of the gas. However, the exact paths of individual molecules do not matter; there are an uncountable number of micro-states that are equivalent at the macro-level, so to change them has no causal implications at the macro-level.

At the same time that causal relations from below are being loosened, emergent laws (laws relating variables at the higher level) are coming to be seen as significant in their own right, not merely as special cases of lower-level laws. "A hierarchical arraying of parts of the physical universe has been *stabilized,* each part with its quasistable ontology and quasistable effective theory, and the partitioning is fairly well understood."[13]

If strict causal reductionism is denied, and autonomous, higher-level laws governing emergent properties and processes are recognized, the door is open to an even more thorough rejection of reductionism: the recognition of top-down or whole-part causation. It is now coming to be widely recognized in a variety of sciences that interactions at the lower levels cannot be predicted by looking at the structure of those levels alone. Higher-level variables, which cannot be reduced to lower-level properties or processes, have genuine causal impact. Biochemists were among the first to notice this: chemical reactions do not work the same in a flask as they do within a living organism. The relatively new science of ecology is based on recognition that organisms function differently in different environments. Thus, in general, the higher-level system, which is constituted by the entity and its environment, needs to be considered in giving a complete causal account.

Donald T. Campbell describes relations within the hierarchical orders of biology as follows:

(1) All processes at the higher levels are restrained by and act in conformity to the laws of lower levels, including the levels of sub-atomic physics.

(2) The teleonomic achievements at higher levels require for their implementation specific lower-level mechanisms and processes. Explanation is not complete until these micromechanisms have been specified.

But in addition to these reductionistic requirements, he adds:

---

13. Schweber, "Physics, Community and the Crisis in Physical Theory," 38.

(3) (The emergentist principle) Biological evolution in its meandering exploration of segments of the universe encounters laws, operating as selective systems, which are not described by the laws of physics and inorganic chemistry, and which will not be described by the future substitutes for the present approximations of physics and inorganic chemistry.

(4) (Downward causation) Where natural selection operates through life and death at a higher level of organisation, the laws of the higher-level selective system determine in part the distribution of lower-level events and substances. Description of an intermediate-level phenomenon is not completed by describing its possibility and implementation in lower-level terms. Its presence, prevalence or distribution (all needed for a complete explanation of biological phenomena) will often require reference to laws at a higher level of organisation as well. Paraphrasing Point 1, all processes at the lower levels of a hierarchy are restrained by and act in conformity to the laws of the higher levels.[14]

CONCEPTUAL DEVELOPMENTS

Campbell acknowledges that "downward causation" is an awkward term for what he is describing. I hope to shed some light on what one really needs to say here by making a detour through some philosophical developments. In so doing, I hope to show why causal reductionism is in some cases impossible, and why, as Sellars argued many years ago, we have to recognize independent causal levels in reality.

A variety of philosophers have used the concept of *supervenience* to attempt to give naturalistic but nonreductionistic accounts of morality and of mental events. Supervenience is a relation between properties of different types or levels such that if something instantiates a property of the higher level it does so in virtue of (as a non-causal consequence of) its instantiating some lower-level property.[15] In such a case the higher-level property is said to supervene on the lower. There is no consensus on the proper definition of *supervenience*, however; I believe R. M. Hare's use is the most enlightening. In connection with moral ascriptions Hare wrote:

---

14. Donald Campbell, "'Downward Causation' in Hierarchically Organized Systems," in *Studies in the Philosophy of Biology: Reduction and Related Problems,* ed. F. J. Ayala and T. Dobzhansky (London: Macmillan, 1974), 179-86; quotation, 180. See also Roger Sperry, *Science and Moral Priority* (Oxford: Basil Blackwell, 1983), chap. 6. For a summary of the literature, see Peacocke, *Theology for a Scientific Age,* chap. 3.

15. See Terence E. Horgan, "Supervenience," in *The Cambridge Dictionary of Philosophy,* ed. Robert Audi (Cambridge: Cambridge University Press, 1995), 778-79.

First, let us take that characteristic of "good" which has been called its supervenience. Suppose that we say, "St. Francis was a good man." It is logically impossible to say this and to maintain at the same time that there might have been another man *placed exactly in the same circumstances* [italics added] as St. Francis, and who behaved in exactly the same way, but who differed from St. Francis in this respect only, that he was not a good man.[16]

In this case the concept *good* supervenes on St. Francis's behavior and that of his imagined double in the sense that their behavior constitutes their goodness. However, a critical ingredient in Hare's understanding is the recognition of the role of *circumstances.* Thus, I define supervenience as follows: for any two properties A and B, where B is a higher-level property than A, B supervenes on A if and only if something's being A in circumstance c constitutes its being B.

To illustrate, consider the act of killing an animal. Depending on circumstances or context, this lower-level, basic act could constitute a variety of higher-level acts: in one circumstance it could be a religious sacrifice; in another, wanton cruelty; in another merely the preparation of food. We can add yet another layer of description, a moral layer. Presumably under most circumstances offering sacrifice is morally good and preparing food is morally neutral, while under any circumstances wanton cruelty is morally wrong. So the property of being an evil act supervenes on the property of being an act of cruelty, and both supervene on the property of being an act of killing.

A related point is that higher-level properties or states are "multiply realizable." For example, there is a variety of different basic acts that are capable of constituting the higher-level act of cruelty (tormenting children, for instance), or of religious sacrifice (grain offerings). We can relate the concepts of *supervenience* and *realization* by saying that there is often a variety of *subvenient* states or properties, each of which is capable of realizing the supervenient state or property.

The value of recognizing both the supervenience relation and the multiple realizability of supervenient states is that together they allow us to understand how properties (actions, events) of a *single* system, but pertaining to *different* levels of analysis, are related to one another. A causal relation is inappropriate (my being cruel to animals does not *cause* me to be morally bad). Nor is identity the proper relation (there are more ways to be morally bad than by the wanton killing of animals, and killing animals is not always wrong).

To expect to undo the reductionist assumptions of the modern period in one short chapter would be unrealistic, but let us see now what light can be shed on the issue by employing the concept of supervenience as herein defined.

---

16. From R. M. Hare, *The Language of Morals* (1952), quoted by Horgan in "Supervenience."

As indicated in the previous section, the *empirical* failure of reductionism to give complete scientific accounts is now fairly widely recognized. The problem, then, is to explain philosophically how it can *fail* to be the case that the causal laws governing the parts also determine the whole. I believe that the answer to this question must go something like this:

Different sciences (or different sub-disciplines within a science) provide descriptions of reality pertaining to different levels of scale or different levels of complexity. These levels of analysis are necessarily related because they are analyses of more or less the same physical systems.

However, properties or event-descriptions at one level are related to properties or event-descriptions at the other level neither by equivalence (identity) relations nor by causal relations, but rather by supervenience relations. This means that (1) in considering the relation between a lower-level property and its supervenient property, there will always be the broader circumstances or context, describable only at the higher level, to be taken into account.

Laws of nature are always statements of relations among variables within a closed or isolated system. That is, there is a tacit *ceteris paribus* clause: "so long as nothing else interferes with the system." Thus (2) the laws of the lower level are only sufficient to describe the lower-level system in isolation from any variable factors pertaining to the higher-level system.[17]

A consequence of (1) and (2) is that the lower-level laws cannot always fully describe relations among supervenient variables. Supervenience (as here defined) involves additional variables that may interfere with the closed system presupposed in applying the lower-level laws. In other words, the reason the laws of physics are not the sole determinant of complex processes is that they apply in isolated systems, and by definition any level that supervenes involves additional variables. Thus, the supervenience relation, as here defined, provides just enough *decoupling* of the levels of description to account for the failure, in some instances, of causal reductionism.

Because it is the context or circumstances involved in the supervenience relation that violates the *ceteris paribus* clause and disrupts the system described by the lower-level laws, we can see the rationale for referring to the phenomenon as "whole-part" causation. Since these circumstances are often only describable at the higher level of analysis, we can also see the rationale for speaking of this failure of reductionism as "top-down" or "downward" causation.

A brief summary may be in order. The reductionist assumption of the modern scientific worldview has turned out to be false in some instances and thus false as a worldview. There are aspects of the nature or behavior of an entity at, say, the biological level that *can* be explained in terms of chemistry, but there are also aspects of its behavior that can be described and

---

17. William Alston makes a similar point in "Divine Action, Human Freedom, and the Laws of Nature," in Russell, Murphy, and Isham, *Quantum Cosmology*, 185-207.

accounted for *only* in terms of higher-level processes, for example, at the level of ecology.

Earlier reductionists would have granted this, but then would have maintained that those higher-level variables could themselves be reduced to (translated into) terms at the chemical level. It is this latter claim that turns out to be false in some (many?) instances. The higher-level concepts are supervenient on the lower-level concepts, not equivalent to them. There is a surplus of meaning in the higher-level terms, relating to context, to larger causal systems, that cannot be captured by means of the lower-level language. So that surplus can never be subject to laws pertaining to the lower level. Hence, while the causal laws at the bottom of the hierarchy set limits within which higher-level systems must function, they are in such cases necessarily insufficient to determine the outcome of higher-level processes. We need to refer to nonreducible laws pertaining to the higher levels in order to understand natural processes and make predictions. So total causal or explanatory reduction was a false hope.

In place of a metaphysical view based on atomism and reductionism, we need to begin explicating a worldview that is holistic in the sense that it recognizes that whole systems and their parts mutually condition one another. Such a worldview will have important implications for conceptions of human beings, of divine action, and of the relationship between science and theology.

RELATING THEOLOGY AND SCIENCE

We saw in Chapter 2 that conservatives and liberals have strikingly different views on the relations between religion or theology and science. Conservatives claim that science and theology ought to be consistent with one another in the ordinary logical sense; liberals have worked out various comity arrangements dividing up the intellectual territory so that science and theology cannot trespass. The liberals' strategies generally have involved claims that religion and science belong to different and "incommensurable" orders and employ different sorts of language and concepts.

Arthur Peacocke, using the notion of the hierarchy of the sciences, has proposed a model for relating theology and science that, I claim, recognizes the value in both the liberal and conservative views. Peacocke proposes that theology be conceived as the science at the top of the hierarchy. He reasons that theology is the intellectual discipline whose subject matter is the relation of God to everything else, both the natural world and the human world. Thus, theology studies the most complex and all-encompassing system possible.[18]

---

18. For a brief account, see Arthur Peacocke, *Intimations of Reality: Critical Realism in Science and Religion* (Notre Dame: University of Notre Dame Press, 1984); for a systematic development, see Peacocke, *Theology for a Scientific Age.*

A consequence of this move is that we can expect the relation between theology and the other sciences to be analogous to the relations among other sciences in the hierarchy. Each science has a subject matter of its own; it makes use of its own particular language, both theoretical concepts and descriptive terms. And for many purposes, each science has its own integrity—its own autonomy from other levels.

If we take theology to be a science in the hierarchy we can say the same things regarding its special subject matter, its distinctive language and concepts, its relative autonomy from the other sciences. This confirms valid points in the liberal view.

However, the sciences have benefited immensely from their relations with other sciences. Reductive explanations have greatly strengthened all of the sciences by *explaining* phenomena that could only be *described* at the higher levels. For example, breaking the genetic code (at the bio-chemical level) allowed for explanations of inherited characteristics that could be described but not explained at the biological level. In the future, we can expect increased progress from exploration of top-down relations among the sciences.

If we take theology to be one of the sciences in the hierarchy, this means that while its focus of interest does not overlap directly with any other science, neither is it isolated from the others. Findings in both the natural and human sciences do have relevance for theology—as the conservatives have recognized.

Explanatory relations would run *in both directions* between theology and the sciences. Throughout the hierarchy of the sciences, questions arise that cannot be answered at the level where they originate but only by referring to a higher level. I have suggested elsewhere that we call these "boundary questions."[19] Some examples: the flourishing or extinction of a species often can be explained only ecologically; many human behavior patterns can be explained only with reference to social factors.

In a similar way questions arise within both the natural and the human sciences that cannot be answered at the level of science itself. These questions call for either a metaphysical or a theological answer. Cosmology raises a number of such questions. The most intriguing such question being discussed presently arises from recognition that the basic constants governing the evolution of the universe since the Big Bang needed to be "fine-tuned" to produce a universe in which life is possible. These constants include the four basic forces: gravity, strong and weak nuclear forces, and electro-magnetism. Other factors include the total mass of the universe, the weights and charges of the sub-atomic particles. If the ratios between any two of these numbers were different, sometimes even by so little as one part in 10^{40}, calculations show that the universe would be

---

19. See Murphy and Ellis, *On the Moral Nature of the Universe.*

radically different; in most cases, no conceivable forms of life would be possible.[20]

These calculations, widely accepted among cosmologists, raise the question, how did it come to be that the universe has just the features it needed for life? There are attempts either to explain away the amazement or to provide scientific accounts, but clearly a theological answer explains the appearances quite parsimoniously: the universe *was* finely tuned to permit the development of life, because this is what God the Creator intended.[21]

Other questions that arise in cosmology but call for answers of a higher order are: What caused the Big Bang? What is the ontological status of the laws of nature themselves? And, of course, there is the ancient question, why is there a universe at all? So theology provides answers (although not the only possible answers) to boundary questions that arise at the "top edge" of the sciences.

However, the sciences also contribute to theological understanding. For example, consider the doctrine of sin. In the fifth century Augustine used the biological account of sexual reproduction of his own day to explain how original sin could be transmitted from Adam to all of his descendants. Note that only Adam's sin was transmitted, even though Eve's was the first sin. This distinction was due to the (mistaken) biological theory that the "seed" was provided entirely by the male.

Contemporary accounts of the apparently innate tendency to sin often include recognition that our evolutionary past has endowed us with drives that once were crucial for survival but now need to be curbed. Note that this is not to claim that original sin is simply identical with primitive drives. Rather, the concept of sin (a theological category involving the transgression of divine law, or the like) supervenes on both moral and biological concepts: acting according to certain biological drives constitutes an immoral act only under certain circumstances, and the immoral act constitutes a sin only under certain further circumstances, such as the fact that it violates God's law.

So despite theology's disciplinary autonomy, we can improve our understanding of both the natural world and of certain theological concepts by means of explanations that cross disciplinary boundaries. However, explanations are often *causal* explanations; the foregoing account of reciprocal explanatory relations between theology and the sciences brings us to the question of divine action.

---

20. See John Barrow and Frank Tipler, *The Anthropic Cosmological Principle* (Oxford: Oxford University Press, 1986); and John Leslie, *Universes* (London and New York: Routledge, 1989).

21. See Murphy, "Evidence of Design in the Fine-Tuning of the Universe"; and Murphy and Ellis, *On the Moral Nature of the Universe*, chap. 3.

DIVINE ACTION

Two quite different (though related) problems confronted modern attempts to give an account of divine action. One was the assumption that God would have to violate or suspend the laws of nature to bring about any *special* divine act (recall that both liberals and conservatives supposed that God acted constantly through the laws of nature). The other problem was the question how God could act in a universe where all causes were believed ultimately to be natural forces if God was not a natural force. In particular, Newtonian physics was believed to account for all natural forces as purely physical in character.

The short answer to the problem of divine action is the following: The first problem was created by the *mistaken* assumption that all causation was bottom-up. Now we recognize as well top-down causation and genuine causal laws at higher levels of the hierarchy of the sciences. These higher-level laws need to be integrated with the lower-level laws but cannot be reduced to them. So it was simply a mistake to suppose that the laws of physics determine all natural events. This leaves us free to speculate that the totality of natural laws, comprising all levels in the natural-scientific and social-scientific hierarchy, are together incomplete. Just as new kinds of entities with their own proper forms of action need to be recognized as we go up the scale of complexity *because we cannot explain the phenomena without recognizing them,* so too divine acts may need to be recognized for a complete account of the direction of natural and human history.

The second problem was created by what Sellars called the billiard-ball picture of matter and by an overemphasis on mechanical causes. Science itself has moved far beyond this conception of natural causation, so the old arguments based on such a picture should no longer stand in the way of belief in special divine acts.

However, we still need to recognize the intrinsic difference between the kinds of action available to physical entities (however much richer today's conception of physical agents may be) and the specific character of divine acts. It is to be expected that God's mode of action will be appropriate to the kind of agent that God is. This was the point of the medieval distinction between primary and secondary causation, and it continues to be upheld in most theological accounts. The critical issue is to avoid reducing God to a mere physical cause, yet to find ways of recognizing that God's intentional action can bring about events above and beyond what could be accomplished merely by holding the (lower-level) natural processes and causes in existence.

Is the short answer adequate?[22] We can certainly make the following negative statement: in light of these two sorts of changes—the nonreductionist conception of the hierarchy of the sciences and the changes in physics since Newton's day—it is no longer the case that we have clear scientific reasons for rejecting claims regarding special divine actions. In a sense this puts us back to square one: as in the early and middle centuries of Christian history, we have no good reasons (philosophical or scientific) to deny special divine actions, and, I would claim, much theological reason to affirm them.

However, in the medieval period, especially after Thomas Aquinas's integration of Aristotelian cosmology into the theological tradition, it was possible to give an intelligible account, in terms of the current science and philosophy, of how conceptions of divine action and natural causation could be integrated. Some theologians and philosophers believe that such an integrative account should be attempted in our own day, using current science. Others reject any such attempt. However, I suspect that these objections are due largely to liberal conceptions regarding the incommensurability of science and theology, which, I suggest, ought to be seen at this point as a *modern* defensive strategy, no longer needed in the new postmodern context.

Among those who seek to integrate scientific and theological accounts of causation there are two prominent strategies. One is Peacocke's claim that God works solely in a top-down manner, influencing the whole of the universe in a way analogous to the way the environment influences an organism, or as the whole person influences his or her own bodily actions.[23] The difficulty with this latter analogy is that it suggests either that God is like the mind or soul of the universe (a dualism that Peacocke rejects), or else a pantheistic view of God and the world.

To avoid such pantheistic tendencies it is helpful to point out that within the natural world, when we move upward from one level to another, it is not the case that the higher level is merely an organization of parts belonging to the lower level. For example, the social level of reality is not merely composed of individuals. In addition to social groups, social realities include constitutions, bank charters, stock exchanges, and so forth.

---

22. My own assessment is that the first problem is solved, but the second one is not, since current science involves conservation of matter and energy, and we still have the (analogous) problem of explaining how God's action is to be reconciled with this principle. I believe that the way ahead involves an emphasis on God's immanence at the quantum level. See Nancey Murphy, "Divine Action in the Natural Order: Buridan's Ass and Schrödinger's Cat," in *Chaos and Complexity: Scientific Perspectives on Divine Action,* ed. Robert J. Russell, Nancey Murphy, and Arthur Peacocke (Vatican City State and Berkeley: Vatican Observatory and Center for Theology and the Natural Sciences, 1995), 325-57.

23. For his most recent account, see Arthur Peacocke, "God's Interaction with the World: The Implications of Deterministic 'Chaos' and of Interconnected and Interdependent Complexity," in Russell, Murphy, and Peacocke, *Chaos and Complexity,* 263-88.

So to place theology as the top-most science in the hierarchy is not necessarily to say that theology is merely the science of the whole of the empirical order. Rather, it is to say that the behavior of the created universe cannot be explained apart from its relation to an additional kind of reality, namely, God.

Still, Peacocke's metaphors or analogies remain just that; they do not account for what Austin Farrer calls the "causal joint," the point at which divine action affects events in the natural world. The *concept* of top-down causation, with its recognition of the reality of higher-level entities, and the necessity of acknowledging them to be genuine causal agents, clears away many obstacles to an account of divine action, but it is the analogy relating levels of causal description (theology is to science in general as higher-level science is to lower) rather than an analogy between God and natural causes (e.g., the human person) that is useful here.

The second strategy for giving an account of the "causal joint" explores quantum physics and seeks to give an account of God's action throughout the natural and human world by means of action at the quantum level (either alone or in conjunction with top-down action).[24] These discussions are promising but as yet inconclusive.

So, despite the fact that nonreductive physicalism has largely been developed by atheists, it turns out to be quite useful for explicating divine action, for two reasons: First, it denies the typical modern assumption that causation in the natural order is all bottom-up. This was the assumption that led to a view of the universe as a closed causal order governed by the inexorable laws of physics, with the ironic outcome that the very laws Christians believed God had created became an obstacle to believing God could enact any special intentions.

Second, the nonreductive physicalists have provided a more robust conception of physical reality itself than the Galilean billiard-ball universe. They have prodded philosophers to take account both of our common-sense knowledge of the complexity of the physical world as well as of the most recent developments in physical theory. Philosophers have yet to take full account of the difference quantum theory makes to conceptions of causation; theologians, especially, need to adjust their accounts of divine action to take account of current science.

BODY, MIND, SOUL, SPIRIT

Some Christians will consider the gains that nonreductive physicalism offers in solving the problem of divine action to be offset by the losses it involves

---

24. See Murphy, "Divine Action in the Natural Order." See also in Russell, Murphy, and Peacocke, *Chaos and Complexity*, George F. R. Ellis, "Ordinary and Extraordinary Divine Action: The Nexus of Interaction," 359-95; Thomas F. Tracy, "Particular Providence and the God of the Gaps," 289-324; and references therein to earlier literature.

concerning the nature of the human person. Many Christians hold a dualist view of the person and assume that such a view is an essential part of Christian teaching. However, as we saw in Chapter 3, the modern worldview made this topic at least as problematic as that of divine action.

Dualism did not present metaphysical problems for Christians in the ancient and medieval periods. The soul was then conceived in either Platonic or (modified) Aristotelian terms; it was one of a class of entities, the forms. In both Platonic and Aristotelian metaphysics matter and form were correlative notions. For Aristotle, the form was the active principle that gives material beings their characteristic powers. One could almost say that the entire metaphysical system was designed to support the concept of the preeminence of the soul.

By the time that the last vestiges of Aristotelian metaphysics had been purged from modern science, the human soul had become an anomaly and was no longer correlative with an appropriate conception of matter. Descartes's conception of the mind (thinking substance) replaced earlier concepts of the soul in philosophical discourse. As mentioned in Chapter 3, the problems in accounting for mind-body interaction were parallel to those in accounting for special divine action: If the body is governed by deterministic laws, how can it also be said to be under the control of the mind or will? If the mind is immaterial, how can it be a cause in the natural world?

The nonreductive physicalist view does not postulate a substance or entity, the mind or soul, as the seat of mental or spiritual powers, but rather attributes mental and spiritual properties to the entire person, understood as a complex physical and social organism. Since mental states or attributes are states of the whole person, no special causal problems arise. This view of mental states as arising from the functioning of the nervous system is consistent with what we know from science about the interactions between brain states and mental states: measurable effects on the central nervous system have psychological consequences; many psychological or mental states have physiological consequences.[25]

The crucial difference between reductive and nonreductive physicalism is that for the reductive physicalists the meaning and efficacy of the mental is an illusion—it is really only the laws of physics that make things happen. For the nonreductive physicalist human beings are more than mere aggregates of atoms, and the activities that we class as mental and spiritual are at least as important to the course of events as the purely physical aspects.

Because the concepts of supervenience and top-down causation have only recently become available, there is still much to be done in order to explain and support a nonreductive physicalist view of the person, both to overcome

---

25. For an excellent account of the psychophysical unity of the person, the impossibility of separating what we think of as mental events from physiological processes, see David Braine, *The Human Person: Animal and Spirit* (Notre Dame: University of Notre Dame Press, 1992), chaps. 8 and 9.

lingering reductionist worries and also to work out the consequences for an account of the spiritual life (most of the work in this area has been done by philosophers of mind, with no interest in the spiritual aspects of personhood).[26]

Christians also need to examine theological and biblical issues. For example, for a nonreductive physicalist there is the question of what happens to the person during the time between death and the general resurrection. However, some biblical scholars argue that the holistic view of the person represented by nonreductive physicalism is much closer to biblical conceptions of the person, which have been submerged for centuries under dualistic, Platonic translations and interpretations of Scripture.[27]

RELATED HOLISMS

I have claimed that the modern view of matter has been atomistic and reductionistic. However, the same can be said of modern views of practically *everything*! It is widely recognized that modern views of social organizations have been individualistic. The human "atoms" are logically prior to the social arrangements into which they "bond." One form of scientific reductionism was the claim, common among modern thinkers, that social realities could be explained entirely in terms of the behavior of individuals.

> The ideas of Newton, Hobbes, and Locke suggested to the social philosophers of the Enlightenment, like Helvétius and Holbach, that individuals in societies were not only analogous to the atomic constituents of physical wholes but were themselves intelligible in terms of a system of quasimechanical, hedonic attractions and repulsions. Given knowledge of the laws of human psychological mechanics, individual dispositions could be molded to a socially consistent pattern by an appropriate set of ideal institutions.[28]

The postmodern replacement for modern individualism recognizes that the social level has an integrity of its own, not reducible to the level pertaining to the individual, and, in fact, social systems condition individual char-

---

26. However, see Braine, *The Human Person: Animal and Spirit*; and Peacocke, *Theology for a Scientific Age*.

27. See, for example, Ray S. Anderson, "Christian Anthropology," in *The Blackwell Encyclopedia of Modern Christian Thought*, ed. Alister McGrath (Oxford: Basil Blackwell, 1993), 5-9; or Ted Peters, "The Physical Body of Immortality," *Center for Theology and the Natural Sciences Bulletin* 15, no. 2 (Spring 1995): 1-20; and idem, "Resurrection: What Kind of Body?" in *Ex Auditu* 9 (1993): 57-76.

28. Stanley I. Benn, "The Nature of Political Philosophy," *Encyclopedia of Philosophy* (New York: Macmillan, 1967), 6:391.

acteristics and behavior. This rejection of pure individualism has consequences for the social sciences, political philosophy, and ethics.[29]

We have already seen that modern epistemology tended to be atomistic, seeking the simplest possible statements of fact—either about the world itself or about inner experiences—to serve as the foundation for all knowledge. Quine's successor position, epistemological holism, specifically rejects the atomistic approach as one of the modern "dogmas of empiricism."

Most philosophical conceptions of language in the modern period have also been atomistic. Before Frege, the atoms were generally thought to be words. It is the words that have meaning, due to their association with individual ideas or with objects or classes of objects, while sentence meaning is a function of its constituents. After Frege the attention shifted to the sentence or proposition and so began the search for "atomic propositions."

In Chapter 5 I referred to postmodern theories of language as "linguistic holism." This is in recognition of Wittgenstein's thesis that language gets its meaning from its use in a language game, and that language games are bound up with forms of life. Thus, meaning is dependent not on the atomic bits of which a sentence is constructed, but rather on the social *wholes* in which it is used.[30]

CONCLUSION

Just as modern thought formed a coherent worldview, with common strategies for understanding—atomism and reductionism—cutting across a variety of disciplines, so we can begin to see the emergence of a consistent postmodern worldview involving science, philosophy of language, epistemology, ethics. I have suggested that one factor tying together developments in all of these areas is the rejection of reductionism through the recognition that the *organization* of the whole makes it (in some sense) more than the sum of its parts; it is an entity in its own right, with its own specific sorts of agency, an agency needed to account for what goes on in the world.

The epistemological changes surveyed in Chapter 4 are widely accepted, and we have seen that they have already had significant impact on a number of theologians and philosophers of religion. This has led to new conceptions of theological method, of the relation between the Bible and theology. It even calls for new formats for systematic theology texts: no longer will they begin with prolegomena called "theological foundations."

---

29. See Alasdair MacIntyre's *After Virtue* for a top-down account of how participation in social practices determines what individual characteristics count as virtues.

30. For a more detailed account of the variety of postmodern holisms, see Murphy, *Anglo-American Postmodernity*, chap. 1.

The revolutionary character of the ideas of Wittgenstein and Austin has been overlooked by many in their own guild, but nonetheless there has been some impact on theologians and philosophers of language, and the influence seems to be growing. Because theories of language tend to be assumed rather than explicit, change in this area should be expected to be slow.

Nonreductive physicalism has been an available option at least since the 1930s. However, it is only now that philosophers are beginning to get clear on how to avoid reductionist conclusions. The "discovery" of top-down causation in science should be expected to increase philosophical interest in this area. Apparently only a few theologians are aware of these developments or of their potential for solving the modern problem of divine action. In addition, much needs to be done to appropriate theologically the radical metaphysical changes called for by quantum theory.

As we saw again and again in the preceding chapters, the issues of theological knowledge and theological language are inextricably tied to conceptions of divine action. Thus, I predict that although significant progress has been made in recontextualizing theology for the postmodern age, no ultimately satisfying theological program will appear without a solution to the problem of divine action.

The theological world needs to "catch up" with A. H. Strong, writing well over a century ago; only now does it have the conceptual resources to make sense of his claims that special divine acts are both revelatory of God's intentions and consistent with the laws of nature:

An event in nature may be caused by an agent in nature yet above nature. This is evident from the following considerations:
(a) Lower forces and laws in nature are frequently counteracted and transcended by the higher (as mechanical forces and laws by chemical, and chemical by vital), while yet the lower forces and laws are not suspended or annihilated, but are merged in the higher, and made to assist in accomplishing purposes to which they are altogether unequal when left to themselves.[31]

We are now at the threshold of being able to explain *how* it is that the laws of the lower level are "merged in the higher, and made to assist in accomplishing purposes to which they are altogether unequal when left to themselves"—including the "laws" of divine-human interaction.

---

31. Strong, *Systematic Theology*, 121.

Conclusion

The thesis of the first half of this book was that modern philosophy limited the options for theologians, resulting in the bifurcation of theology into two types. While many theologians sought middle ground between the liberal and conservative tracks, in fact there was never any consistent third way.

However, the modern positions creating these limited options have all been overturned. I attempted to show in the second half of this book that a new philosophical world is coming into view. Consequently, this is an exciting time to do theology (as well as to engage in other academic disciplines). One reason is that writers today are aware of their own philosophical assumptions in ways that their recent predecessors have not been. When one is working in the midst of a worldview or philosophical era, the constitutive assumptions of the worldview are, as Huston Smith suggests, like the glasses on one's nose. We who are living through a change in worldview are made aware of the glasses because we see them change before our eyes.

A second reason for excitement is that today's theologians have an opportunity to think out afresh the most basic assumptions of their own field. We have seen samples of theological moves that employ the new philosophy. However, there is much room for creativity. Lindbeck and Thiemann have not had the last word on postmodern theological method; McClendon and Smith have not had the last word on postmodern theories of religious language; nor Peacocke on divine action.

My projection (and hope) is that theologians from both left and right will find resources in the new worldview for many fresh starts in theology—not fresh starts in content so much as fresh approaches to issues of method, to conceptions of the nature of the theological task. And these new approaches ought to form more of a continuum or spectrum of theological options than a dichotomy.

We have seen in Chapter 4 that if an epistemological theory something like MacIntyre's is adopted, it becomes *impossible* for theologians to choose between Scripture and experience as the foundation for theology. Scripture has its authoritative and ineliminable role in the tradition as the formative text. However, it is impossible to do theology except in light of current experience if what one wants to do is to *apply* the text in one's own context. So one might expect theologians of both liberal and conservative leanings to find this model acceptable, perhaps to see that it allows them to acknowl-

154

edge truths about their craft that could not easily be enunciated with the resources of foundationalist philosophical language.

The methodological moves of the Yale school are fairly consistent with a MacIntyrean model. However, these theologians are criticized by both conservatives and liberals (especially by "revisionist theologians" such as Tracy): the conservatives see them as relativists; the revisionists see them as fideists. This shows that the important question to resolve is the second-order epistemological question: not, How do we justify belief *x* given the Christian framework? but rather, How do we speak intelligibly to those in other frameworks? How can we justify our framework when we recognize the existence of competing frameworks? I have claimed that Lakatos and MacIntyre have, if not complete solutions, at least important insights to offer. These need further exploration. Theology's success as a discipline answerable both to the church and to the academy depends on an answer to this second-order epistemological question. An important ingredient will need to be the development of a theory of truth appropriate to the new epistemology.

We have seen in chapter 5 that an Austinian theory of language makes it clear that happy religious language must ordinarily be both representative and expressive. Both the postliberals and current conservatives such as Donald Bloesch have recognized this in their own way, although without the clarity of the analysis by McClendon and Smith. However, despite agreement on the principle that speech acts have essential representative and affective dimensions, theologians may still differ in the relative importance they assign to each in particular instances.

A most interesting locus for philosophical developments is in the understanding of biblical interpretation. I have argued that an Austinian speech-act approach would incorporate and orchestrate the various current forms of biblical criticism. It seems that Frei's and Lindbeck's post*liberal* accounts of narrative interpretation—reversing the *direction* of interpretation—should be of great interest to conservatives, who have often complained that rendering the texts into modern categories has been reductionistic.

However, in both theological argumentation and biblical interpretation there is a tension between fidelity to the authoritative texts and applicability or relevance in the current context. We should expect basic tendencies toward conservatism and liberalism to continue to appear in theologians' decisions about how to proceed when such tensions appear in specific instances. Yet this should result in a spectrum of theologies rather than bifurcation.

Ronald Thiemann has recognized that the coherence of the postliberal theological program depends on a more robust doctrine of divine action (prevenient divine acts in revelation and salvation history) than most modern liberal theologians have been willing to countenance. In this instance he agrees with what conservatives have maintained throughout the modern period. If the conceptual problems that drove liberals to reject straightforward accounts of special divine acts can be solved (and I have argued that the resources are now available to do so), then the successors of both liberal and conservative theology can agree on the *concept* of special divine action, although there may be a range of views on the extent or frequency of such action. Postmodern evangelicals will likely argue for frequent interactions between God and the believer; postliberals may claim that God's acts are limited to those of great significance to salvation history.

I have already described the hierarchical ordering of theology and the sciences as a compromise between liberal views of the autonomy of theology and conservative views of the intersection of theological and scientific truth claims. This new view of the relation between theology and the sciences, combined with the change just mentioned in conceptions of divine action, would dramatically change the debate over evolution. It would be possible to claim (with the liberals) that God is acting in and through all natural processes, including the evolutionary process, *and* to raise the question (as do some conservatives) whether the ordinary processes involving both law and chance are adequate, without special divine action, to account for the appearance of humans. However, if there were such special acts they would necessarily be invisible to science, because they would not be violations of natural laws. The divine action would be supervenient on states describable at the biological level in biological terms—the criterion for an act of God is not, on this new model, the absence of a scientific account. As a supervenient discipline, theology can answer questions that arise within science but cannot be answered by science alone. For example, evolutionary theory can account for the development of species with improved survival value, but it cannot account for the fact that natural history has produced species of higher value on *non*-biological scales of value. It certainly cannot explain why the process should result in a species capable of a relationship with God.

So, at the dawn of this postmodern age in the Anglo-American intellectual tradition, there are serious philosophical problems to be addressed. The two that seem the most pressing are: (1) solution to the second-order epistemological question; and (2) making good on the promise of new views of science, causality, and the relations among the disciplines for the purpose of integrating theological accounts of divine action with knowledge of the world.

However, the possibilities for developments that are radically *new* in philosophical terms and at the same time a *recovery* of the fullness of Christian truth are too plentiful to mention. And there appears to be the opportunity for an ecumenical move, more important to the peace of the church in our day than interdenominational discussions: healing the painful and contentious rift between Christians of the left and the right.

Index